MANAGING THE IMBALANCE
From Burnout to Breakthrough

I0518343

J. McCarthy, PhD, MBA

RL♀
Real Life Series Publishing

Managing the Imbalance: From Burnout to Breakthrough
Reclaiming Your Time, Energy, and What Matters Most

For permissions, inquiries, or bulk orders, please contact:
rlspublishing@gmail.com

This book is intended for informational and inspirational purposes only. It
is not a substitute for professional advice. The author and publisher make
no guarantees regarding the results that individuals may experience from
the information provided.

Published by The Real Life Series Publishing Co., LLC
www.thereallifeseries.com

Printed in the United States of America
First Edition, July 2025

ISBN:979-8-9989754-0-0
Library of Congress Control Number: 2025910950

DEDICATION

Before you turn these pages, I want to share a brief story.

Imbalance was a learned behavior, etched into my DNA like an inherited blueprint from my late mother. The workaholic tendencies began in my teenage years and spanned into adulthood. It was common for me to work multiple jobs, always burning the candle at both ends, until my body finally declared this pattern was no longer sustainable. Illness forced me to surrender my relentless pace, and my resources (a concept we'll explore deeply throughout this book) emerged in profound and unexpected ways.

To my family, friends, and my basketball community (parents, teammates, former players)...

Your prayers, out of state visits, meals, and countless acts of kindness created the foundation for healing. I offer my deepest gratitude. Though you are too numerous to name individually, know that every gesture remains imprinted on my heart.

To my wife...

Your unwavering faith transformed our darkest days. You were my prayer warrior, my steady anchor, the quiet miracle behind every recovery. You held our family together while nursing me back to health and faced every obstacle with a grace that defies words.

To my children...

Thank you for stepping up when I couldn't. I'm sorry for scaring you, and grateful for the quiet strength you showed while helping your mother hold everything together.

This book is dedicated to all of you who quite literally carried me when I could no longer walk this path alone. May this book be the same lifeline for someone else that you were for me.

TABLE OF CONTENTS

THE NUMBERS SPEAK

Burnout, stress, and imbalance are not just personal struggles, they're widespread challenges affecting millions. In this book, each chapter begins with a compelling statistic, shedding light on the prevalence and impact of these issues. These data points are more than numbers; they represent real people facing real challenges. As you read, may these insights affirm your experiences and inspire your journey toward balance and well-being.

The Balance Journey

Burnout isn't just personal fatigue; it's a public health crisis. According to the American Psychological Association (2023), 77% of Americans reported experiencing work-related stress in a recent survey, with nearly three in five reporting that it had a negative impact on their personal lives. Meanwhile, the World Health Organization now classifies burnout as an occupational phenomenon affecting millions worldwide.

Yet this crisis isn't distributed equally across generations. Recent studies reveal an alarming trend: younger workers are significantly more susceptible to burnout. Research shows that 84% of Gen Z individuals report experiencing burnout, compared to 74% of Millennials and just 47% of Baby Boomers (Forbes, 2024). Another study found that almost half (48%) of individuals aged 18 to 29 reported feeling consistently drained, compared to 40% of their peers aged 30 and older (CNBC, 2024). This stark contrast is a reminder that burnout doesn't wait for midlife to strike; it's affecting our workforce earlier and more severely than ever before.

Behind these statistics are real people: parents missing bedtime stories, young professionals questioning their purpose before they've even established their careers, and individuals of all ages sacrificing health for achievement. This isn't just about being tired; it's about losing connection to what matters most. Perhaps you've felt it too, that moment when everything seems both urgent and impossible. This book begins by identifying what's really happening beneath the surface of your overwhelm.

When I began researching work-life balance, I never imagined how personal this journey would become. As a father of eight, a coach, and someone who has personally experienced the devastating effects of burnout, I've witnessed firsthand how the pursuit of "having it all" can leave us with nothing left to give.

This book is for you if:

- You're excelling at work but feel like you're failing at home
- You've tried countless productivity systems but still feel overwhelmed
- You're physically, mentally, or spiritually exhausted from trying to meet competing demands
- You want practical strategies, not just inspirational platitudes

- You're early in your career and already feeling depleted, wondering if this is simply "how it is"

- You're mid-career and struggling to balance achievement with presence

What sets this approach apart is its whole-person perspective. We'll address not just your calendar, but your identity. Not just your time management, but your energy allocation. Not just your boundaries, but your beliefs.

This isn't a book about perfect balance... that doesn't exist. It's about managing the imbalance; choosing where to focus in each season with clarity and purpose, without sacrificing what matters most.

Throughout our journey together, we'll move beyond simply identifying these challenges to developing practical strategies that shift your experience from surviving to thriving. The insights, tools, and principles you'll discover in each chapter will ultimately converge into what I call the IMBALANCE™ Method. This is a comprehensive nine-step framework designed to help you reclaim your time, rebuild your strength, and restore your purpose without losing yourself in the process.

You'll see elements of this method woven throughout our exploration: how to identify what's draining you, establish boundaries that protect your peace, align your actions with your values, and nurture the relationships that matter most. Each chapter builds toward this unified approach that transforms scattered strategies into a cohesive system you can rely on daily.

In Chapter 16, you'll receive the complete IMBALANCE Method implementation guide, but the foundation for lasting change begins now, with your willingness to examine what isn't working and your commitment to creating something better.

The balanced life you're seeking isn't just possible, it's within your reach. Let's begin building it together, one intentional choice at a time.

The Silent Struggle

Begin by identifying the invisible burdens, hidden drains, and nonstop pressures that make balance feel impossible, even when you're giving it your all.

CHAPTER 1

Where it All Begins

According to the National Alliance on Mental Illness, 82 percent of employees were at risk of burnout in 2024, with women, young professionals, and mid-level workers especially impacted.

How It Started

I grew up in a single-parent home during a time when the saying "it takes a village" wasn't just a saying, it was a way of life. This upbringing not only shaped my childhood but also my understanding of community.

Back then, neighbors could discipline you, call your parents, and have a full report delivered before you even made it back to your porch. And you'd get in trouble all over again; not because you embarrassed your parents, but because they cared. That was the world I came up in: one filled with aunties and uncles who weren't related by blood but by responsibility.

My village included church members, coaches, scout leaders, martial arts instructors, teachers, and, most of all, my grandparents. They didn't have much but gave me everything I needed: love, structure, and perspective.

As a child, I was a quiet observer. What I saw most consistently was my mother, strong, composed, and seemingly unshakable. She worked the night shift from 11 p.m. to 7 a.m., cared for her aging parents during the day, and still managed to find time for her church and community activities. She was always in motion, always giving, always showing up.

There's a memory I'll never forget. One Sunday morning, on the way to church, our car caught fire. I watched a small flame flicker through the narrow gap where the hood met the car, followed moments later by thick clouds of ominous black smoke.

Most people would panic. My mother calmly got my grandmother and me out of the vehicle, called for help, and made arrangements to get us to the service, as if it were just another moment in the day. I can only imagine the breakdowns she had when she was alone, yet in front of me, she was grace under pressure.

Looking back, I'm in awe of how much she carried. At one point, she held two full-time jobs, working 80 hours a week, while still being there for her family, friends, and faith. Her schedule was packed, and her plate was overflowing, but she kept going.

Until she couldn't.

At just 46 years old, my mother suffered a stroke. The weight of her commitments to her children, her parents, her church, and her community caught up with her. Like many caregivers, she gave endlessly but rarely paused to refill her own cup. These warning signs of burnout and imbalance will become clearer as we explore the pressure points that affect modern work life in the chapters ahead.

Looking back now, with adult eyes, I see what was invisible to me then. However, as a young man, I didn't understand it. I questioned why she didn't slow down. Why didn't she prioritize herself? As I aged, I realized the mark she left. People loved her.

Every time someone told me how much my mother meant to them, I felt a surge of pride. She was mine. Her example became my blueprint for balance and sacrifice. That was until I became a father myself and realized the blueprint needed to be updated.

What It Looks Like Now

I start with her story because our pasts shape our patterns. What we grew up seeing becomes what we expect from ourselves, even when it's unsustainable.

As a father of eight, I carry my mother's lessons with me. But I'm also intentional about rewriting some of the rules she adhered to. There have been cultural shifts since her era, yet specific pressures remain constant.

The world has changed. Today's workplace doesn't look like the one my mother knew, and that's not necessarily a good thing. Technology keeps us constantly connected. Emails, texts, and deadlines follow us home and haunt us on weekends. Job loyalty is down. Stress is up. And the lines between work and family time? Blurred at best.

At home, it's not much calmer. You've got school updates, practice schedules, meal planning, bedtime routines, and all of that's before you've had your first sip of coffee. You're trying to excel at work and be present for your loved ones, but your body is tired. Your brain is fried. Your soul feels stretched thin.

You're doing everything… and it still doesn't feel like enough. Maybe you've let go of your own goals, telling yourself, "One day." Maybe you're haunted by what could've been. Or perhaps you're just trying to make it to Friday without breaking down.

You're not alone. Whether you're a parent juggling family responsibility, a young professional starting your career, or someone managing multiple personal passions alongside work, these same questions of balance and fulfillment remain.

My mother once dreamed of starting her own daycare and going back to school. She earned her associate's degree, but she aspired to something more. I wonder if my mom had the tools we have today, such as online courses and flexible jobs, would things have been different? Would she have lived longer? Would she have lived better?

The Cost

The truth is, life is heavy. And if you're not careful, it will carry you instead of the other way around.

That's why I wrote this book. Not because I have all the answers, but because I've lived the questions. I've struggled with the same imbalance. I've felt the guilt of missing moments. I've battled burnout while trying to be everything to everyone. And I know what it's like to succeed on paper and still feel like you're failing at home.

So, what's the solution?

There's no magic fix. No one-size-fits-all strategy. However, there *are* things you can do, tools you can use, to shift from barely surviving to intentionally thriving.

This book is part reflection, part roadmap. It combines research and practical strategies to help you achieve peace with your priorities and live a more fulfilling, balanced life. We're not striving for perfection, just better.

Throughout our journey together, we'll move beyond simply identifying these challenges to developing practical strategies that shift your experience from surviving to thriving.

Throughout this journey, I will reveal what I call the IMBALANCE™ Method… a framework of nine principles designed to help you reclaim your time, rebuild your strength, and restore your purpose without losing yourself in the process. Yes, I use the word 'imbalance' intentionally, because perfect balance doesn't exist. What exists is the skillful management of imbalance, and that's exactly what we'll learn together. We'll unpack this together as you move through each chapter.

Let's begin.

Personal Reflection Questions

1. Think about someone who modeled work-life patterns for you growing up. What habits or beliefs did you inherit that might be affecting your approach to balance today?

2. When was the last time you felt truly present and at peace? What elements were in place that made that possible?

3. If you could rewrite one aspect of your daily routine to better align with your values, what would you change?

4. What story do you tell yourself when you can't "do it all"? How might reframing that narrative change your experience?

Action Steps

- *Schedule a Life Audit:* Block 30 minutes this week to list all your current commitments and responsibilities. Mark which ones energize you and which ones drain you.

- *Create a "Not Now" List:* Write down goals or activities you value but need to temporarily set aside. This isn't saying "no forever"… it's saying "not during this season."

- *Establish a Daily Pause:* Identify one 5-minute window each day where you can pause, breathe, and reset. Put it in your calendar as a non-negotiable appointment with yourself.

- *Share Your Intention:* Tell someone you trust about one small change you're committed to making. External accountability increases follow-through by nearly 65%.

This journey begins with understanding. Before we can transform our relationship with work, family, and self, we need to recognize the unseen forces that make balance seem so elusive. In the next chapter, we'll explore why this struggle feels particularly challenging in today's world and why even our best efforts sometimes fall short.

CHAPTER 2

Why It Feels So Hard

The American Psychological Association (2023) reported that 77 percent of U.S. workers experienced work-related stress in the past month, with more than half saying it harmed their health.

Understanding the Root of Imbalance

Before we can fix something, we must understand what is causing it to break. The constant tug-of-war between work and family isn't just about poor time management or not trying hard enough. It's about systems, expectations, and unspoken pressures that weigh heavily, even when we can't quite put them into words.

Let's unpack what's really going on behind the imbalance.

The Pressures We Inherit

Even though the world has changed, the expectations haven't caught up. These inherited expectations form the foundation of our struggles.

Traditionally, men were expected to provide for the family while women managed the household. And although many families now rely on two incomes, and plenty of men are deeply involved fathers, the *pressure* to "do it all" hasn't gone away. If anything, it's gotten worse.

We live in a hustle culture that applauds being constantly busy. Somewhere along the way, we started treating burnout like a badge of honor. Long hours? That means you care. Skipped family time? That means you're committed. Exhausted? Good. That means you're working hard enough. But when success comes at the cost of our well-being, who's really winning?

Stress Isn't One-Size-Fits-All

Understanding this personalized nature of stress reveals why solutions can't be universal. Two people can be facing the exact same challenge, and only one feels completely overwhelmed. Why? Because how we *perceive* stress matters just as much as the stress itself. Researchers talk about three layers:

Stressors - the external pressures (e.g., deadlines, bills, sick kids)

Perceived stress - how we interpret those pressures

Strain - the toll it takes on our body, mind, and relationships

Think about two different parents. One has a flexible job, a supportive partner, and a trusted babysitter. The other has a rigid schedule, an unsupportive partner, and no one they can trust with their kids. Both parents have the same parental responsibilities, but they have very different experiences.

Context matters profoundly in how we experience pressure. This is why comparing your life to others is unfair and unhelpful. We all carry different weights, and some of us do it with less help.

This gap between objective demands and our subjective experience of them explains why balance appears differently to each person and why we require personalized approaches rather than one-size-fits-all solutions. Whether you're balancing childcare and a career, managing the demands of early career advancement, caring for aging parents, or pursuing personal goals alongside professional growth, your unique context shapes your experience of pressure.

When Stress Becomes Burnout

Burnout doesn't arrive with a warning. It sneaks in through the cracks of long days, sleepless nights, and suppressed frustration. You stop feeling motivated. You stop feeling present. You stop feeling like *you*.

Burnout affects your body, your mind, your confidence, and yes, your relationships. When you're emotionally drained from work, it's hard to show up fully at home. The people who need you most often get what's left over.

This is especially common in professions that require emotional labor, such as coaching, teaching, counseling, healthcare, and ministry. You spend so much time pouring into others that there's nothing left in the tank.

The Power of Support (and the Pain of Its Absence)

If you've ever felt like you're carrying everything alone, you're not imagining it. Real, consistent support makes a huge difference. A helping hand, a listening ear, a "Hey, I've got dinner tonight" can be the thing that keeps someone from breaking.

Studies show that individuals with strong support systems tend to feel less stressed, manage their responsibilities more effectively, and experience fewer negative effects of burnout. Yet here's the catch: not everyone has that network.

Many professionals, especially those who lead others, feel *expected* to be strong, to keep it together, and to never ask for help. Isolation is dangerous; it creates shame, and it makes the imbalance feel permanent. You weren't meant to carry all this alone.

Now That We Know Why, Let's Talk About How

Understanding the *why* doesn't fix the problem, but it does give us clarity and help us name what we're really facing. Now, we can start building tools.

Let's explore real strategies for creating better boundaries, managing stress, and finding small ways to reclaim your peace, even in a demanding world. It's not about perfect balance. It's about better choices.

Personal Reflection Questions

1. What cultural or family expectations about work and achievement do you find yourself trying to live up to? Which ones no longer serve you?

2. Consider a recent stressful period. What resources (personal, social, organizational) were missing that could have made it more manageable?

3. When do you find yourself comparing your capacity to others? What would happen if you honored your unique stress threshold instead?

4. What would your life look like if you prioritized well-being as much as achievement?

Action Steps

- *Map Your Support Network:* List the people who genuinely support you. Next to each name, note how they help (practical assistance, emotional support, perspective). Identify any gaps in your support system.

- *Challenge One "Should"*: Identify one expectation you've placed on yourself that's creating unnecessary pressure. Practice saying, "I don't have to..." and complete the sentence.

- *Create a Stress Response Plan:* List three healthy ways you can respond when stress peaks (e.g., a specific breathing technique, a quick walk, a supportive person to call).

- *Schedule a Mind Clearing Session:* Designate 15 minutes daily journaling about anything weighing on your heart or mind, then let it go. This helps clear mental space for what matters most.

Now that we've examined the broader pressures and expectations that create imbalance, it's time to look deeper at what's happening beneath the surface. Understanding why it feels hard is just the first step; identifying what's actually depleting your resources is where real change begins.

In the next chapter, we'll examine exactly what depletes your energy and how to protect your most precious resources. Let's explore what truly drains you and how recognizing these energy leaks can transform your approach to achieving a work-life balance.

CHAPTER 3

What's Really Draining You

Approximately 65 percent of U.S. workers say their job is a very or somewhat significant source of stress (Occupational Safety and Health Administration, n.d.).

The Hidden Drains on Your Energy

Managing work and family life often feels less like balance and more like a juggling act with fire. This constant shuffling leaves many feeling perpetually exhausted. Nonetheless, the issue isn't just about how many hours are in your day, but rather what those hours are costing you.

To understand this imbalance, let's examine the key frameworks that contribute to it. Don't worry, we're not going full textbook here. These concepts might sound academic, but they explain exactly why you feel drained, stretched, and one calendar reminder away from collapse.

Frameworks

Let's distinguish between four key frameworks that explain why balance feels so elusive and what's really draining you:

- The *Conservation of Resources (COR) Theory* serves as our primary framework, explaining how stress occurs when resources are threatened or depleted. This model shows why you feel drained when demands exceed your available resources. We will explore this further.

- Building on this foundation, *Social Expectation Theory* examines the external pressures that society, culture, and organizations establish, influencing our behavior. These expectations often create impossible standards that no individual could realistically meet, yet we internalize them as personal failures.

- *Perceived Stress Theory* complements this by emphasizing our internal interpretation of pressure. This framework illustrates how two individuals can encounter identical circumstances yet exhibit distinct stress responses, depending on their perception and available resources.

- Finally, *Role Conflict Theory* specifically examines how competing identities, such as professional, parent, and partner, create internal tension when the demands of one role interfere with the performance of another.

Understanding these distinct frameworks helps us see that work-life imbalance isn't just a personal failing; it's a complex interaction between resource depletion, societal structures, personal perception, and role expectations. Let's dive deeper into Conservation of Resources Theory, which forms the backbone of our approach.

Conservation of Resources: The Foundation

Research provides valuable insight into why we feel so depleted. Especially when we're doing everything "right" but still feel overwhelmed. According to the Conservation of Resources (COR) Theory, stress occurs when our personal resources are threatened, lost, or not sufficiently replenished (Hobfoll, 1989). These "resources" aren't just material possessions; they also include intangibles such as time, energy, peace of mind, and meaningful connections. Think of these as personal reserves that can be depleted or replenished.

Think of these like internal "bank accounts." Every meeting, errand, expectation, late-night email, and obligation makes a withdrawal. And when those withdrawals exceed your available reserves, without consistent deposits, burnout begins to take root.

COR theory helps us understand why burnout isn't about weakness or poor planning. It's about resource imbalance. The model also explains why people in the same situation can feel entirely different; one person may have more resources or more opportunities to recover than the other.

Further deepening this experience is Social Role Theory, which highlights how societal expectations about work, gender, and performance shape our internal stress responses (Eagly & Wood, 2012). When external demands clash with internal values or perceived limitations, role conflict intensifies. You may feel guilty for setting boundaries or anxious when you can't meet unrealistic norms.

Together, these theories help us name what's often felt but rarely said: burnout is rarely caused by "too little grit" and far more often by too many withdrawals from systems that never pause to pour back in. If you keep spending without replenishing, you become emotionally overdrawn. When you operate on empty, even the smallest things can feel overwhelming.

When Work Steals Too Much

Let's say you're working 60+ hours a week. You're giving it your all. But at the end of the day, there's nothing left for your spouse, your kids, or even yourself. You're not imagining that tension. That's a resource drain, and it's one of the core drivers of burnout.

COR theory explains that work-family conflict occurs when the resources your job demands leave too little for what matters at home. You're not failing, you're just running low on what helps you thrive.

Types of Resources

Not all resources are money or time. Some are internal. Some are emotional. All are valuable. Let's break it down:

Personal Resources

- Your energy, your health, your emotional bandwidth
- Things like rest, confidence, spiritual peace, and mental clarity

Social Resources

- The people who show up for you: your spouse, your kids, friends, coworkers, mentors
- People who say, "I've got you," when you're at your limit

Organizational Resources

- Support from your workplace: flexible schedules, paid time off, understanding supervisors
- The systems that either help you manage life or make it harder

The balance of these resources determines your resilience in facing life's demands. When you have these resources in place, you're more resilient.

More grounded. More capable. However, what happens when those resources are scarce? That's when the cracks start to show.

Understanding what drains your resources is the first step in what we'll later explore as the **IMBALANCE** Method... Identifying what depletes you so you can protect what matters most.

Let's Clarify a Few Things

Before we go deeper, here are a few terms we'll refer to throughout the book. Let's make sure we're on the same page:

- *Work-Life Balance*: Being able to meet your responsibilities at work without sacrificing your personal health or relationships.

- *Work-Family Conflict*: When your job and your family life feel like they're competing, and nobody's winning.

- *Resource Drain*: The feeling of having nothing left to give because work has taken it all.

- *Burnout*: Physical and emotional exhaustion caused by long-term stress. You're still doing the things... but you don't feel anything while doing them.

- *Social Support*: The people you can call at 2 AM. The ones who bring food, take the kids, or just let you vent. They matter more than you think.

Why This Matters

This chapter isn't just about theory; it's about *awareness*. You can't manage what you don't understand. Now that you know what's draining you and what fills you back up, you can begin to make intentional decisions that protect your peace, your energy, and your time. Because here's the truth: It's not always about doing *less*. Sometimes, it's about making sure what you *do* gets you more of what matters.

Personal Reflection Questions

1. What activities or interactions consistently leave you feeling depleted? What patterns do you notice?

2. Which of your personal resources (energy, time, emotional capacity) feels most compromised right now?

3. What boundaries have you struggled to maintain, and what makes enforcing them challenging?

4. If you could eliminate one energy drain from your life tomorrow, what would make the most significant difference?

Action Steps

- *Conduct an Energy Audit:* Track your energy levels hourly for three consecutive days, noting activities that either boost or drain your energy. Look for patterns and consider restructuring your day to align with your natural energy cycles.

- *Implement One Energy Shield:* Identify one boundary you'll establish this week (e.g., no work emails after 7 PM, no phone during meals) and communicate it clearly to those affected.

- *Practice Resource Replenishment:* Schedule one activity specifically designed to replenish your most depleted resource, such as taking a walk in nature for mental clarity or connecting with a friend for emotional support.

- *Delegate One Task:* Identify something you can delegate or eliminate entirely that's currently consuming your time or mental bandwidth.

With a clearer understanding of our resources and what depletes them, we can now address one of the most challenging aspects of modern life: persistent pressure. For many, the stress isn't occasional… it's constant. And when pressure never lets up, even the strongest among us begin to crack.

These insights about resource protection become especially crucial in workplace environments, where external pressures often conflict with our need for sustainable balance. In the next chapter, we'll examine what happens when stress becomes chronic and how to protect yourself when walking away isn't an option.

CHAPTER 4

When the Pressure Doesn't Let up

Workplace stress is estimated to contribute to 120,000 deaths each year in the United States (Goh, Pfeffer, & Zenios, 2016).

The Reality of Constant Pressure

You might've told yourself, "This is just a busy season." We all tell ourselves stories to make it through difficult periods. The reality is, it's been a long season, and you're starting to feel it.

You're not lazy. You're not broken. You're just tired. And not the kind of tired that goes away with a nap. This is deeper. This is the tiredness that sits in your bones and makes even the simplest things feel heavy.

That's the kind of pressure we're dealing with.

Workplace Stress: The Weight We Carry

Work doesn't stop at the office anymore. Even after you clock out, the mental load continues. Dinner gets interrupted by Slack messages. Weekends are cluttered with notifications. And while flexibility was supposed to be a perk, it often means your job follows you everywhere.

According to the Centers for Disease Control and Prevention (CDC, 2022), Americans are working more hours than ever, and it's not just physical labor; it's the emotional and cognitive toll of being constantly accessible. For many professionals, especially those balancing caregiving roles, the boundary between personal time and professional responsibility has blurred to near invisibility.

Some pressure is motivating. It helps us rise to the occasion, meet deadlines, and unlock creativity. That's known as *eustress*, or positive stress; a term coined by endocrinologist Hans Selye (1975). But when stress becomes chronic, relentless, and internalized, it shifts into *distress*; a toxic form that quietly corrodes health, morale, and emotional stability.

What Burnout Really Looks Like

Burnout doesn't always wave a red flag. It whispers. You missed a meeting. You forgot a deadline. You snap at your spouse. You feel numb during moments that once brought you joy.

Burnout wears many faces:

- *Physically*: You're tired all the time. Your body hurts. You're more prone to getting sick.

- *Emotionally:* You feel irritable, anxious, or just… disconnected.

- *Mentally*: Your focus is gone. Your motivation is gone. You can't make decisions, and when you do, they feel forced.

Sound familiar? It's not just "part of the job." It's not weakness. It's a warning sign. Your body and spirit are asking for help. These warning signs look remarkably similar whether you're a seasoned professional, a new graduate entering the workforce, a parent, or someone pursuing meaningful work while balancing personal responsibilities.

Why This Happens: The Invisible Culture of Overwork

Workplace culture doesn't always say "burn yourself out." But it often rewards people who do. Companies value the early bird, the late worker, the one who says "yes" to everything. But there's rarely applause for setting boundaries, taking time off, or saying, "I can't take this on right now."

If your job has:

- Constant pressure to be available

- Little to no flexibility

- A lack of support from leadership

- Unclear expectations

…then stress is baked into your work life. Now add in personal obligations, parenting, caregiving, bills, relationships, and the pot boils over.

How to Cope (Without Falling Apart)

Your circumstances may have constraints, but your response remains within your control. You might not be able to quit your job tomorrow. You might not have help at home right now. However, you *can* start making small adjustments to your approach to managing the load.

Let's break it down:

Adaptive Coping (Healthy Tools)

- Exercise – Not just for fitness. Movement helps regulate stress.
- Mindfulness – Even 5 minutes of deep breathing helps reset your nervous system.
- Time management – Not just a planner. Prioritize what actually matters today.
- Boundaries – Create a "shutdown" time for work, and protect it.

Maladaptive Coping (What to Watch For)

- Avoiding people or tasks
- Overindulging in food, alcohol, or scrolling
- Withdrawing emotionally
- Ignoring physical health

These aren't character flaws; they're red flags that something deeper needs attention.

You're Not Meant to Do This Alone

Research indicates that individuals with strong social support networks tend to experience less burnout. That means having someone to vent to, cry with, or just sit in silence with.

If you've been trying to do this alone to carry the weight silently, it's time to invite help. Ask a friend to check in. Talk to a mentor. Open up to your partner. Or say yes to professional support.

Burnout doesn't mean you're weak. It means you've been strong for too long without a break.

And About That Phone...

Technology was supposed to make life easier. Instead, it made you reachable 24/7. If your boss can message you at 9 p.m. and expect a reply, or if you check email "just real quick" at your kid's soccer game, the line between work and life is gone.

Reclaim it...

- Silence notifications after hours.
- Keep work apps off your home screen.
- Use tech for *your* benefit, not your employer's convenience.

The Goal Isn't Perfection, It's Awareness

You might not be able to change your workplace overnight, but you *can* start making different choices. Recognize your warning signs. Protect your peace. Speak up. Rest, not just when you're finished, but when you're fading.

We'll continue exploring how stress and imbalance affect individuals differently and why women, in particular, often bear a heavier burden in both work and home.

We're not here to shame. We're here to shift. Let's keep going.

Personal Reflection Questions

1. What physical or emotional warning signs has your body been sending that you might be ignoring?

2. When was the last time you truly disconnected from work? What made it possible or impossible?

3. What beliefs do you hold about rest and productivity that might be contributing to burnout?

4. What aspects of your workplace culture encourage unhealthy relationships with work, and how might you navigate them differently?

Action Steps

- *Create a Shutdown Ritual:* Develop a 5-minute end-of-workday routine that signals to your brain that work is done (e.g., writing tomorrow's priorities, clearing your desk, a brief walk).

- *Designate Tech-Free Zones:* Identify one physical space in your home and one time period each day that will remain device-free.

- *Schedule Recovery Time:* Block out 30 minutes this week specifically for a restorative activity that has nothing to do with productivity.

- *Practice Saying No:* Script and rehearse kind but firm responses to requests that exceed your capacity.

As we've seen, workplace pressure affects everyone, but its impact isn't uniform. Our identities, roles, and social expectations all shape how we experience and respond to stress. Nowhere is this more evident than in the complex dynamics of motherhood.

While workplace pressures affect everyone, they pose unique challenges for parents, particularly women, a topic we'll examine as we explore how different life stages require different balancing strategies. In the following chapter, we'll explore how both working mothers and stay-at-home mothers navigate unique challenges in their pursuit of balance, purpose, and well-being.

Section II

Identity, Expectations & Energy

Explore how identity, expectations, relationships, and time affect your energy, your peace, and your purpose. Understand the personal dynamics behind burnout.

CHAPTER 5
The Mom Dichotomy

Working mothers are nearly 70 percent more likely to experience burnout than stay-at-home moms, while stay-at-home moms report higher levels of depression (Great Place to Work & Maven, 2020; Talkspace, 2023).

Beyond the Motherhood Divide

The motherhood debate has created unnecessary division among women. Let's stop pretending there's a right way to "do" motherhood. Whether you're climbing the career ladder with a diaper bag on your shoulder or navigating toddler tantrums in between loads of laundry, the truth is the same: Motherhood is work. And it's hard.

This chapter isn't about who has it worse; it's about naming the silent pressures that both working and stay-at-home moms carry. The goal is not to judge or divide, but to understand and heal the tension mothers often feel within themselves... and toward each other.

The Working Mom: The Balancing Act No One Prepares You For

The experience of working mothers combines professional demands with parental responsibilities in a way that creates unique challenges. For many women, working outside the home isn't a luxury; it's a necessity. For others, it's part of their identity. Either way, being a working mom means constantly doing mental gymnastics to be present and effective at both work and home.

The Guilt That Never Quite Leaves. You kiss your child goodbye and rush off to a meeting, but your heart's still in the daycare pickup line. You're chasing goals and paychecks but also asking yourself, *"Am I missing too much?"* Research backs this up. Many working moms report higher stress levels and intense feelings of guilt, especially when societal expectations still paint the "ideal mom" as someone always available, always selfless, and always home.

The Unspoken Pressure at Work. It's called the motherhood penalty, the notion that mothers are perceived as less committed at work, even when their performance proves otherwise. So what do most women do? They overcompensate. Say "yes" to everything. Stay late. Skip lunch. Show up even when they're barely holding it together. And when the office closes? The second shift begins.

The "Second Shift" Is Real. Even when both parents work full-time, women still carry the majority of household and childcare duties. That's not just inconvenient, it's exhausting. And it's why burnout hits moms hard. This double burden creates the exact resource drain we explored earlier, particularly impacting emotional energy reserves that are crucial for both work and family life.

The Stay-at-Home Mom: A Different Kind of Exhaustion

Working mothers face the constant juggling act of professional demands and family responsibilities. But what about those who have chosen to focus primarily on home? The challenges may look different on the surface, but beneath lies a surprisingly similar struggle.

Both working and stay-at-home moms share the fundamental challenge of balancing competing demands on their finite energy and attention. The difference lies not in whether this tension exists, but in how it manifests. Let's explore the unique challenges that stay-at-home mothers face in finding equilibrium and recognition in their vital role.

Depending on One Income Isn't Always a Choice. Financial dependence is real. For many women, stepping away from the workforce means giving up more than just a salary; it's a shift in identity, security, and future options. The pressure builds if the relationship isn't stable or the financial plan isn't solid. Sociologist Arlie Hochschild refers to it as the unpaid job at home. Stay-at-home moms may not clock in, but they never clock out. Their jobs have no office, no weekends off, no paychecks, and often, no breaks at all.

The Loneliness You Don't Talk About. While working moms deal with meetings and co-workers, stay-at-home moms often spend their days surrounded by little people with big emotions and very few adult conversations. It's easy to feel unseen. Isolated. Forgotten. Research shows that stay-at-home moms often report higher levels of loneliness and depression.

The Battle for Self-Worth. In a world that celebrates resumes and promotions, it's hard not to feel like you're "just a mom." And while others may praise your sacrifice, they don't always understand it. Stay-at-home moms often feel the need to explain or justify their decision, even to themselves.

Stop Comparing. Start Understanding

There's been quiet tension between working moms and stay-at-home moms for decades. But it's not because one has it better. They're both stretched thin, and society hasn't caught up with the support they deserve.

Upon closer examination of both experiences, we find more commonalities than differences. So let's stop asking, *"Who has it harder?"* and start asking, *"How can we make it easier for everyone?"*

What is needed:

- *Real Policies That Actually Help.* Mothers need policies that acknowledge their reality: flexible work options that don't force an impossible choice between presence and paychecks; affordable childcare that makes returning to work financially viable; and comprehensive paid family leave that allows for crucial bonding time without sacrificing job security.

- *A Cultural Shift.* Mothers don't owe the world an explanation. Choosing to work? That's valid. Choosing to stay home? Also valid. Raising the next generation is a lifetime's work, whether you do it in heels, sneakers, or slippers.

- *A Stronger Sisterhood.* Less judgment and more empathy. Less "How do you do it all?" and more "How can I support you?" Whether it's playdates, group chats, or venting over coffee, connections are vital. And when moms support each other, we all win.

Perfection

There's no perfect mom. There's the mom who's doing her best with what she has. The one who shows up... tired, hopeful, messy, and full of love. That's you.

So whether you're in boardrooms or living rooms, with spreadsheets or snack trays, you matter! Your work matters... your peace matters. And in this book, we'll keep fighting for a life where your health, your dreams, and your family can coexist, not compete.

Personal Reflection Questions

1. What judgments or assumptions have you internalized about your choice to work or stay home with children?

2. Where do you feel the most guilt in your motherhood journey, and what would happen if you released that guilt?

3. What support do you most need right now that you're not receiving?

4. How might you extend more grace to mothers making different choices than yours?

Action Steps

- *Create a "Done Well" List:* End each day by writing three things you did well as a parent, regardless of what wasn't perfect.

- *Schedule Connection Time:* Plan one meaningful connection with your child each day, even if it's just 10 minutes focused on them.

- *Form an Alliance:* Reach out to another mother with a different work situation than yours and plan a coffee date to share perspectives without judgment.

- *Request Specific Support:* Identify one concrete way someone could help you this week, and ask for that help.

The motherhood journey reveals how profoundly our identities influence our experience of balance or burnout. While parenting responsibilities shape our daily schedules, our deeper relationships, both at home and at work, ultimately determine whether we experience meaning amidst the chaos.

These dynamics extend beyond parenting. Our relationships, career choices, and personal values all affect how we distribute our time and energy. In the next chapter, we'll examine the connection between who we are, why we work, and who we love, and how these elements form the foundation of either fulfillment or exhaustion.

CHAPTER 6

Who You Love, and Why You Work

According to McKinsey & Company (2019), nearly half of married couples in the U.S. are in dual-career households, reflecting the growing challenge of balancing love and labor.

You can have a stacked resume, a steady paycheck, and a list of accomplishments that make people clap, but if the people closest to you feel unseen, unheard, or forgotten, does it really matter?

Work-life balance isn't just about calendars and boundaries; it's about relationships and reasons. It's about who you're doing all this for and whether they still feel connected to you at the end of the day.

Relationships: The People Who Pay the Hidden Price

The Cost You Didn't Count

Balance isn't just about what you're doing; it's also about what you're missing. The late meetings. The business trips. The quick "I'll be home soon" that turns into missed bedtime stories.

Every yes to something at work is, by default, a no to something else. That's not always bad, but when it becomes the norm, people notice. Especially the ones who love you.

You may be providing for them, but are you *present* for them? What does it gain you to be respected in the world if your household resents you? Provision isn't just financial; it's an emotional, physical presence that shows up when it's inconvenient, not just when it's scheduled. This principle applies whether those important people are your children, friends, parents, or members of your broader community.

Leadership Pull vs. Family Pull

If you're in a leadership role, in your job, your church, or your community, the pull to serve others can feel never-ending. You tell yourself, "I'm doing this for my family," but your family may not feel that way.

Without intentional effort, leadership can become an excuse, a way to justify absence while missing the emotional deposits your people actually need. We assume others know our hearts, but sometimes, they just see our schedule. This tension between professional responsibilities and family needs creates the same resource drain we discussed earlier in the book, depleting your emotional energy in both spheres unless it is managed intentionally.

Let's pause for a moment and reflect on these competing demands. Before moving forward, consider:

- Which of these tensions resonates most strongly with you right now?

- How has this tension manifested in your life this past week?

- What would better alignment look like, specifically for you?

Now, let's continue exploring how understanding your deeper motivations can transform these tensions from conflict points to opportunities for integration.

A Lesson from the Backseat

There was a time when I would scold my younger kids for constantly letting the car window shade down. Then one day, my older son was driving, and I experienced motion sickness when the shade was up. Sitting in their seat that day taught me a valuable lesson: perspective matters.

When it comes to relationships, we must stop assuming others understand our side. Sometimes, we have to sit where they sit, feel what they feel, and ask ourselves honestly, *"What does my love look like from their point of view?"*

Motivation: What's Really Driving You?

What motivates you to get up early, stay late, and push through exhaustion? For most of us, it's a mix of survival, ambition, purpose, and legacy. Albeit sometimes, we're chasing goals that don't align with the life we say we want.

Our motivations often run deeper than we realize. Our upbringing, cultural expectations, and personal experiences shape them. Some of us work tirelessly to provide the financial security we never had as children. Others pursue achievement to prove their worth or to leave a lasting impact.

Understanding these deeper drivers helps us distinguish between motivations that energize us and those that deplete us. When our work aligns with our core values, even challenging days feel purposeful. But when we're driven by fear, comparison, or others' expectations, no amount of success truly satisfies.

When Loss Rewrites Your Why

If you've ever lost someone, you know, it changes everything. Suddenly, the "someday" goals don't feel good enough anymore. You realize how much time you traded chasing titles or finishing projects while letting the most important relationships coast on autopilot.

That awareness hurts, but it can also heal. It gives you the chance to realign your drive with your values.

Ask yourself:

- Why am I working so hard?

- Who benefits from this grind, and who suffers?

- Am I building the life I want or the one I think I *should* want?

Aligning Your Life from the Inside Out

You don't have to give up your ambition, but it's time to make sure your ambition doesn't come at the cost of your peace. This alignment between your values and actions is central to what we'll call the **A** in our IMBALANCE Method... ensuring your priorities truly **A**lign with what you say matters most

Here's how to start:

1. *Clarify Your Priorities.* What are your non-negotiables? Family dinner? Mental health days? Time with your kids? Write them down. Schedule around them, not over them.

2. *Communicate with Intention.* Let the people in your life know what you're working on *and why*. Include them in your goals, but don't make them guess where they stand.

3. *Integrate, Don't Separate.* Take your kids to career day. Invite your spouse to that conference dinner. Let your professional world see your personal life; it builds empathy on both sides.

Building Stronger Connections
Relationships thrive on effort, not perfection. Here's how to keep them growing, even in the hustle…

Prioritize Presence Over Perfection
Your loved ones don't need you to be flawless; they just need you to *be there*. You don't have to say the perfect thing. Just show up. Quality time doesn't have to be elaborate to be meaningful.

When you're mentally and emotionally present, even during ordinary moments like dinner conversations or bedtime routines, you communicate that nothing is more important than the person in front of you. Remember that children and partners often measure love by attention and availability, not achievements or perfection.

Practice Empathy and Real Listening
Be curious about their experience. Ask how they're doing. Don't just defend your choices, hear their feelings. Authentic listening means setting aside your agenda and fully immersing yourself in their world, even if only momentarily.

Make eye contact, put away distractions, and ask follow-up questions that demonstrate your genuine engagement. When someone shares a struggle, resist the urge to offer solutions immediately. Sometimes people simply need to be heard and understood. The simple act of validating another's experience… "That sounds really difficult," or "I can understand why you feel that way"… builds deeper trust than any advice could.

Make Room for Connection
Making room for genuine connection requires intentional effort in today's busy world. Put connection time on the calendar just like you would a meeting, giving it the same level of commitment and priority. When you're with family, unplug completely; your phone can wait, and those emails will still be there tomorrow.

Small things matter tremendously; simple texts, handwritten notes, and random "just thinking of you" messages can go a remarkably long way in nurturing your relationships. These seemingly minor gestures communicate that despite your busy schedule, the people you love remain at the forefront of your thoughts.

Remember your work matters, but your people matter more. You can be successful and still be present. You can chase big dreams and still come home for dinner. It just takes clarity, commitment, and the courage to say, "Enough. I need better." Let's build better... together.

Personal Reflection Questions

1. Who are the people most affected by your work habits and schedule? What would they say about how present you are in their lives?

2. What's one relationship that has suffered because of your work commitments? What specific steps could you take to begin healing that connection?

3. When you think about your "why" for working so hard, whose faces come to mind? Are your actions aligned with what those people truly need from you?

4. What fear keeps you saying "yes" to more work when your relationships need more of you?

5. If you had only one year left to live, would your current work-life balance reflect the legacy you want to leave?

Action Steps

- *Conduct a Relationship Audit:* List your key relationships and assess the quality of each one honestly. Note specific areas needing attention.

- *Schedule Connection Time:* Block out non-negotiable time each week for the people who matter most. Treat these appointments with the same importance as work meetings.

- *Create "No Phone Zones":* Designate specific places (such as the dinner table or bedroom) or times (6-8 pm) where devices are put away to facilitate genuine connection.

- *Write Your "Why" Statement:* Create a clear, specific statement about why you work and what truly matters in your life. Keep it visible in your workspace.

- *Have the Tough Conversation:* Identify one relationship that has been suffering due to your work habits and initiate an honest conversation about how to improve it.

Now that we've examined who we're doing all this work for and why, let's turn our attention to the most precious resource we have in managing our lives: time itself. In the next chapter, we'll explore how time, our most limited resource, either strengthens or strains these vital relationships that give our work meaning.

CHAPTER 7

The Complexities of Time

Gallup polls show that nearly half of Americans feel they lack enough time for what they want each day, and over 60 percent of working adults report chronic time stress (Gallup, 2015; Gallup, 2023).

Redefining Your Relationship with Time

Time. We want more of it, we fear losing it, and sometimes, we waste it without even knowing why. You're not lazy. You're not failing. You're human, trying to navigate life's demands with limited hours and limitless responsibilities.

So, let's stop blaming the clock and start reshaping our relationship with time.

Time Is More Than a Schedule

As a child, I was fascinated by time travel; the idea that you could undo a mistake with one well-timed move. Now, as an adult with a full house and a overflowing plate, I know we can't change the past. However, we can change how we show up today.

Time is a resource, and how we spend it reflects what we value. That's why managing time isn't about squeezing in more tasks. It's about making sure the right things get the best of you, not just what's loudest or most urgent.

What's Your Relationship with Time?

Before diving into techniques, pause and ask yourself: How do I treat time?

Why we misuse it...

- *Fear of failure:* Sometimes we procrastinate not out of laziness, but fear. We avoid hard things because we're afraid of not doing them well.

- *Exhaustion:* When your tank is empty, even a 5-minute task can feel like climbing a mountain.

- *Fear of running out of time:* Ironically, being overwhelmed by time slipping away can stop us from using it well.

Sound familiar? You're not alone.

The Value of Time in Relationships

What you give your time to is what you're saying matters most. Some people work crazy hours, yet their families still feel loved because they're intentional with the little moments: a text, a check-in call, a quick prayer, or a note. It doesn't have to be grand, it just has to be real.

In my own house, with eight people and eight different personalities, I've learned that connection comes from presence, not perfection. A few minutes of intentional time is more powerful than hours of distracted multitasking.

Time Management Strategies That Actually Work

Managing your time effectively isn't just about productivity; it's about protecting those relationships we discussed in the previous chapter. Every 'yes' to work during family time communicates a priority, whether we intend it or not. This isn't about doing more. It's about protecting your peace and prioritizing what actually moves you forward.

1. Prioritization: What Really Matters?

Ask yourself daily: *What's truly important?*

- Identify your top three priorities for work and home.
- Distinguish between "urgent" and "important."
- Learn to say no to things that don't align with your values.

2. Time Blocking: Give Everything Its Place

Don't wait for time to appear magically. Assign it.

- Block work time for deep focus (and guard it).
- Schedule family time like a meeting, and show up fully.

- Carve out space for yourself: rest, reflection, recreation.

3. Boundaries: Protect Your Time Like a Paycheck

Time leaks occur when you fail to protect it.

- Set clear work hours and honor them.
- Turn off notifications during family time.
- Create tech-free zones in your home. Let people *feel* your presence.

4. Delegation: You Weren't Meant to Do It All

You don't get extra credit for doing everything alone.

- At work: Delegate where possible. It builds trust and frees your bandwidth.
- At home: Invite your family to contribute. Kids can clean. Partners can cook. You're not the only capable one in the house.

5. Goal Setting: Make It Manageable

Big dreams are powerful, but overwhelming goals lead to stalled progress.

- Use the IMBALANCE Method for goal-setting.
- Break big goals into micro-steps.
- Celebrate progress, not just completion.

6. Self-Care: You Can't Pour from Empty

Burnout wastes more time than rest ever will.

- Prioritize sleep, nutrition, and movement.
- Schedule downtime. Literally.
- Do what fills your soul: reading, walking, prayer, music, stillness.

7. The Power of Intentionality

Practice doing nothing for 5 minutes a day. Sounds silly? It's actually powerful. It teaches you to:

- Be present.
- Get quiet.

- Hear what matters.
- Resist the lie that your worth = your productivity.

Time Is a Mirror

The way you spend your time reflects who you believe you are and what you think matters. Don't let your calendar tell a story you don't believe in. Don't spend so much time building a life that you forget to *live* it.

This chapter isn't about mastering your minutes. It's about managing your meaning, reclaiming control, and choosing rest, valuing presence.

You have time. Let's learn to use it like it's sacred.

Personal Reflection Questions:

1. What activities consistently drain your time without contributing value to your life or goals?

2. When was the last time you felt truly present, without thinking about what's next on your to-do list? What made that moment different?

3. Which of your current time management habits are reactions to guilt or fear rather than intentional choices?

4. If you were to gain an extra hour each day, what would you spend it on? What does this reveal about what might be missing in your current schedule?

5. How does your relationship with time affect the people closest to you?

Action Steps:

- *Track Your Time:* For one week, record how you spend your time (not how you think you spend it). Look for patterns, time leaks, and alignment with your priorities.

- *Implement Time Blocking:* Create a template for your ideal week, allocating specific blocks for deep work, family, self-care, and other priorities.

- *Set Digital Boundaries:* Configure "Do Not Disturb" settings on your devices during your most important personal and work times. Communicate these boundaries to others.

- *Practice Saying No:* Identify three upcoming requests or opportunities you should decline because they don't align with your priorities, and practice declining graciously.

- *Create a "Done List":* At the end of each day, write down what you accomplished rather than just focusing on what's left undone. Celebrate progress, not just completion.

While managing our time is crucial, it means little if our minds aren't properly nurtured to make thoughtful decisions about how we spend those precious hours. The way you manage your mental landscape directly affects how effectively you utilize your time and how present you are while doing so.

As we transition from understanding the problems to building solutions, we must first attend to the foundation of it all, our mental, physical, and spiritual health. The healing work begins with nurturing these core aspects of ourselves, creating internal resources that will fuel the external changes we seek.

Let's turn our attention to nurturing the control center that coordinates all these aspects of balance: your mind. In the next chapter, we'll explore how to restore your mental clarity and resilience as the first step toward comprehensive renewal.

SECTION III

The Healing Work

---

*Reclaim your wellness and reset your inner life with
practical tools to nourish your mind, body, and spirit—
because burnout recovery starts from the inside out.*

CHAPTER 8

Nurturing Your Mind

More than 9 million U.S. adults reported using meditation in the past year, and nearly two-thirds said it helped significantly with stress and anxiety (National Center for Complementary and Integrative Health, 2023).

The Power of a Nurtured Mind

Your mind is your greatest tool, but also the most vulnerable. It holds your memories, fuels your choices, and narrates your daily life. And in a world constantly demanding more of you, at work, at home, in your head, it's easy to neglect the very thing that holds it all together.

Let's change that. Let's get intentional about nurturing your mind so it can serve you, not sabotage you. This healing work represents the **M** in our **IMBALANCE** Method... nurturing your **M**ind, body, and spirit as the foundation for sustainable balance.

The Power of Perception

Have you ever heard the saying, *"Perception is reality"*? Two people can face the exact same moment, such as a job loss, a breakup, or a traffic jam, and walk away with two completely different experiences. Why? Because our mindset filters our reality.

The Stories We Tell Ourselves

If you believe life is out to get you, you'll see evidence of that everywhere. However, if you train yourself to find lessons, even in failure, you gain wisdom, not wounds.

I used to tell my older sons, *"I did everything wrong that I possibly could, so just do the opposite of what I did, and you'll be alright."* That came from a place of regret. As I grew, I realized my mistakes weren't just missteps, they were milestones. They shaped my creativity, resilience, and perspective. I didn't fail. I learned.

You can do the same. Just as our perception shapes our experience of time, it also determines how we show up in our relationships. The stories we tell ourselves have a profound impact on everyone around us.

Shifting Negative Thinking

Changing your mindset doesn't happen overnight, but it can start today. Try these...

- *Reframe the story* - Instead of "I messed up," say, "I learned something."

- *Challenge negative thoughts* - Don't let your brain lie to you. You are not your worst moment.

- *Speak life over yourself* - Your words matter. If you say you're defeated long enough, you'll live like it.

- *Surround yourself with positive voices* - Surround yourself with people who build you up, not tear you down.

Laughter Is Mental Medicine

When was the last time you laughed really laughed? Laughter isn't just a mood-booster; it's science. It lowers stress hormones like cortisol. It triggers feel-good chemicals like endorphins. It gives your brain a break from constant overthinking.

Ways to laugh more:

- Watch your favorite comedy or memes (guilt-free).

- Spend time with people who make you belly-laugh.

- Laugh at yourself. Don't take life (or your mistakes) too seriously.

- Create moments of joy with your kids, your partner, or your friends.

You don't need perfect circumstances to find joy; you just need permission.

Mindfulness: Training Your Focus

Your mind runs all day, but rarely sits still. Mindfulness teaches you to slow down, breathe, and regain control over your thoughts and emotions.

It's not about ignoring problems; it's about facing them with clarity instead of chaos.

Try this:

- *Deep breathing*: Inhale for 4, hold for 4, and exhale for 4. Repeat.
- *Thought observation*: Let your thoughts come and go like passing clouds. No judgment.
- *Stillness sessions*: Sit in silence for 5 minutes. No phone. Just presence.

Even five minutes a day can recalibrate your mind and regulate your stress.

Mental Toughness

Real strength is forged through time and adversity. It's demonstrated not in avoiding life's challenges, but in how you rise after being knocked down. Mental toughness shines brightest in your recovery from disappointment and your choice to move forward even when feeling overwhelmed.

Signs of mental strength:

- You make decisions based on values rather than fleeting emotions
- You sit with discomfort instead of seeking immediate escape
- You bounce back from setbacks with genuine resilience
- You maintain composure when others around you panic

Want to build this inner fortitude? Challenge yourself daily in small but meaningful ways. Wake up earlier than usual. Face a lingering fear. Disconnect from technology for an evening. These seemingly minor victories gradually stack into lasting mental toughness that serves you through life's inevitable storms.

Resilience That Respects Your Humanity

Mental toughness in the context of burnout recovery isn't about forcing yourself to "push through" or "grit your teeth." This misunderstanding actually perpetuates burnout. Instead, true mental toughness combines two seemingly opposite qualities:

1. The courage to face difficult realities and make challenging decisions

2. The compassion to acknowledge your human limitations and needs

This balanced approach to mental fortitude means making decisions based on values rather than fleeting emotions, sitting with discomfort rather than avoiding it, bouncing back from setbacks with genuine resilience, and maintaining composure during stressful situations; all while respecting your need for rest, support, and renewal.

Mental toughness isn't denying your humanity; it's embracing it with wisdom and self-respect.

Tetris: The Game of Balance

Tetris is one of my favorite puzzle games. I play to detox, and liken it to life. You're constantly trying to fit all the pieces (work, family, and goals) into the limited space of your day. You are continually adjusting, stacking strategically, and attempting to clear clutter.

If you're lost, Tetris is a classic game where blocks of different shapes descend from the top of the screen. The goal is simple… arrange these pieces efficiently to create complete rows that disappear, giving you more space and points.

Life works remarkably like Tetris in several specific ways:

1. *Pieces come whether you're ready or not:* Just as Tetris sends blocks at an ever-increasing pace, life delivers challenges and opportunities on its own schedule.

2. *Strategic placement matters:* In Tetris, randomly dropping pieces creates chaos. Similarly, without planning, the demands of work and family land haphazardly, creating gaps and instability.

3. *Clearing complete rows creates space:* In the game, completed rows disappear, giving you breathing room. In life, fully completing tasks (rather than leaving them half-done) creates mental and emotional space.

4. *Adaptability is crucial:* As the game progresses, you must adjust to different shapes and speeds. Life similarly requires flexibility as circumstances change.

5. ***Panic leads to poor decisions:*** When Tetris speeds up, panic often causes players to place pieces randomly. In life, stress can similarly lead to reactive rather than strategic decisions.

The lesson? Just as successful Tetris players think ahead, adapt quickly, and remain calm under pressure, managing life's demands requires strategic planning, adaptability, and emotional regulation; skills we're developing throughout this book.

Forgiveness: The Key to Mental Freedom

You cannot nurture a healthy mind while carrying the weight of unhealed pain. These emotional burdens consume mental energy that could otherwise fuel your creativity, joy, and presence with loved ones. The process of release begins with acknowledging how much space unforgiveness occupies in your life.

Forgive others. Forgiveness isn't saying, "It's okay." It's saying, "I won't carry this pain forever." Resentment is heavy. Let it go. When you forgive, you're not changing the past; you're changing its power over your present. This doesn't mean reconciling with everyone who's hurt you; it means freeing yourself from the emotional tether that keeps you bound to that pain.

Forgive yourself. You can't be present in the now if you're stuck in shame about the past. You did the best you could with what you knew. Now that you know better, you can do better. Self-forgiveness isn't about excusing mistakes; it's about creating space for growth. Treat yourself with the same compassion you would offer a friend who's struggling with regret.

Forgetting What Doesn't Matter

Just as we often forget our dreams by morning (dream amnesia), we sometimes hold onto memories that no longer serve us, and forget the ones that do. Our minds have limited capacity, yet we often fill them with unhelpful ruminations, outdated worries, and narratives that keep us small. Psychological research shows that intentionally practicing selective attention, focusing on what serves your wellbeing, physically reshapes neural pathways over time.

Ask yourself:

- Is this thought helping me or hurting me?
- Do I need to keep replaying this story?

- What do I want to remember instead?

Let your mind release what it no longer needs, and hold onto what gives you hope. This isn't about denial or toxic positivity; it's about consciously curating your mental landscape. This practice is especially crucial for younger professionals who face the added pressures of constant connectivity and comparison through social media, where the boundary between personal worth and professional achievement often blurs.

Final Takeaways

The health of your mind fundamentally determines how you experience everything in your life, from your most challenging workday to your most precious family moments. These key principles aren't just nice ideas; they're practical tools for transforming how you navigate your daily journey:

- *Your perception shapes your life. Change the lens, change the outcome.* The stories you tell yourself about your circumstances often have a greater impact than the circumstances themselves. Choose interpretations that empower rather than diminish you.

- *Laughter is healing. Seek it. Share it.* Joy isn't just an emotional state; it's medicine for your mind and body. Make space for lightness, even during the heaviest seasons. The physiological benefits of genuine laughter include reduced stress hormones and enhanced immune function.

- *Mindfulness is muscle-building. Train it every day.* Like any skill, present-moment awareness strengthens with consistent practice. Even five focused minutes daily builds the capacity to remain centered during life's inevitable storms.

- *Like Tetris, keep adjusting and clear clutter strategically.* Life will continuously send challenges your way. Success isn't about avoiding them but about strategically arranging them and clearing away what's unnecessary before overwhelm sets in.

- *Forgiveness is freedom. Let go.* Every grudge, resentment, and self-criticism you harbor occupies mental real estate that could otherwise be used to fuel creativity, connection, and growth. Release to make room for what matters.

- *Avoid negative thoughts.* Negative thinking patterns create neural pathways that become increasingly automatic. Consciously redirect your thoughts toward constructive perspectives, focusing on possibilities rather than limitations.

Your mind can either drain you or drive you; the difference is how you take care of it. These aren't simply self-improvement techniques; they're the foundation for sustainable balance across every domain of your life. When your mental landscape is well-tended, everything from work decisions to family connections benefits from your clarity and presence.

Let's continue to cultivate the mindset that creates the life you deserve. Remember that this work isn't about perfection; it's about consistent, compassionate attention to the thoughts that shape your experience.

Personal Reflection Questions:

1. What negative thought patterns most consistently undermine your peace or progress?

2. When faced with failure or setbacks, what story do you typically tell yourself? How could you reframe this narrative?

3. What brings you genuine laughter and joy? How long has it been since you prioritized these things?

4. In what situations do you find your mind most at peace? What elements of those moments could you incorporate into your daily routine?

5. What one mental habit would most transform your quality of life if you could change it today?

Action Steps:

- *Start a Thought Journal:* For one week, record negative thought patterns and identify their triggers. Next to each, write a more balanced perspective.

- *Schedule Joy:* Put at least three activities that bring you genuine laughter or happiness on your calendar for the coming week.

- *Practice Daily Mindfulness:* Commit to 5 minutes of mindfulness practice each day. Use a timer and focus on your breath or a simple meditation.

- *Create a Mental Detox Plan:* Identify media, relationships, or habits that consistently drain your mental energy, and create a specific plan to limit their impact.

- *Forgiveness Exercise:* Write a letter (you don't need to send it) releasing yourself or someone else from past hurts that have been weighing on your mind.

A healthy mind requires a healthy vessel to house it. Let's shift our focus from nurturing your thoughts to caring for the body that carries them. We'll explore how physical well-being forms the other half of this vital foundation.

CHAPTER 9

Caring for Your Body

Women and men benefit from regular exercise, though women may achieve the same gains in half the time. Exercise lowers premature death risk across genders (National Institutes of Health, 2024).

Your Body as Your Foundation

Your body is the vessel that carries your purpose, your passion, and your presence. However, too often, in the busyness of life, it's the first thing we neglect.

We say we'll eat better tomorrow, sleep more on the weekend, and start exercising when life slows down. But what if your body isn't something to maintain *later*? What if it's the foundation for how you show up in every part of your life today?

Let's talk about caring for your body, not out of guilt, but out of love.

The Mind-Body Connection

When your body is out of alignment, everything else feels harder:

- Low energy leads to short tempers.
- Poor nutrition fogs your brain and drains your motivation.
- Lack of movement makes stress build up like pressure in a valve.
- Inconsistent sleep steals your creativity, patience, and peace.

As we've just explored, mental and physical health create a continuous feedback loop, each one reinforcing or depleting the other. You can't pour from an empty cup, and your body is that cup. Take care of it, and it'll take care of you.

Movement: A Daily Act of Self-Respect

Why Movement Matters

» Exercise isn't just for athletes. It's a mental health tool, a stress-relief valve, and a way to show up stronger for your family and yourself. Even just 20–30 minutes a day can:

- Boost your mood and focus

- Improve heart and brain health

- Help prevent chronic illness

And no, it doesn't have to happen in a gym.

Movement That Fits Your Life

» Finding movement that suits your unique lifestyle makes consistency more achievable. Start simple with these everyday opportunities:

- Take the stairs

- Do push-ups on the kitchen counter

- Walk during your kids' practice or your lunch break

- Stretch before bed

- Dance in your living room

The key isn't intensity, it's consistency.

Nutrition: Fuel, Not Just Food

Eat to Function, Not Just to Fill

» In today's fast-paced world, we default to what's easy, but convenience often comes at the cost of nutrition:

- Processed food spikes your energy, only to crash it

- Sugar and caffeine give false fuel

- Poor eating habits lead to inflammation, irritability, and fatigue

Your food is your fuel. Make it count.

Easy Nutrition Upgrades for Busy Days

» Small, practical changes to your eating habits can have a major impact on your energy levels throughout the day. Try incorporating these simple upgrades:

- Add protein to every meal. It keeps energy steady.

- Stay hydrated. Fatigue often disguises itself as dehydration.

- Keep healthy snacks on hand, such as nuts, fruit, and protein bars.

- Prep ahead. Smoothies, crockpot meals, overnight oats.

One change at a time: Swap chips for fruit. White bread for whole grain. Soda for water. Don't overhaul your diet overnight. Think sustainable. Think small wins.

Rest: The Most Underrated Power Move

Meaningful rest isn't just about physical recovery; it creates the space for mental clarity and emotional resilience we discussed in the previous chapter.

Why Sleep Is Non-Negotiable

» Sleep isn't lazy, it's leadership. It's recovery. It's a mental reset. It's emotional regulation. Without proper rest, you:

- Make poor decisions

- Struggle to focus

- Get sick more often

- Become more reactive at work and at home

Sleep Smarter, Not Just Longer

» Prioritize rest the way you would a major meeting. Quality matters as much as quantity when it comes to restorative sleep. Implement these evidence-based practices to enhance your sleep quality:

- Go to bed and wake up at the same time each day.

- Shut screens down an hour before bedtime.

- Create a calming routine: prayer, journaling, stretching,

reading.

- Cut caffeine after 2 pm.

Active Recovery Is Still Rest
  » Recovery isn't just sleep. It's how you reset after stress Recovery is rest for the soul:

    - Light stretching

    - Nature walks

    - Breathing exercises

    - Quiet time without a screen

My Journey

Just as I shared in Chapter 1 about my mother's experience with burnout, I've walked this path myself. There was a period when I wore exhaustion like a badge of honor. I believed that pushing through, skipping sleep, and grabbing whatever food was available was just "part of the hustle." But the more I neglected my body, the more everything else started to fall apart: my patience with my children, my presence with my spouse, my creativity in my work.

Life forced me to slow down. This neglect eventually culminated in serious health consequences that forced me to reevaluate everything. The change didn't happen overnight, but small, consistent adjustments, such as drinking more water, walking daily, and prioritizing sleep, transformed not just how I felt physically, but also how I showed up in every role in my life. I didn't just feel better; I *was* better. As a husband. As a father. As a leader.

You deserve to feel good in your own skin. You deserve to have energy for the people and dreams that matter to you. Don't wait for your body to sound the alarm. Take charge now, before life forces you to.

Key Takeaways

Remember: taking care of your body isn't selfish, it's strategic. It's the foundation for everything else... including the Consistency over perfection we'll explore as part of your complete balance framework.

These principles aren't about perfection or achieving an ideal body type; they're about creating the physical foundation that supports everything else in your life. When your body thrives, your capacity to handle life's challenges expands dramatically.

- *Move daily* —> even if it's just 10 minutes.
- *Eat to fuel* —> not just to satisfy a craving.
- *Rest on purpose* —> sleep is sacred.
- *Start small* —> and stay consistent.
- *Adapt to your life stage* —> whether you're facing early career demands, navigating a single lifestyle with its unique pressures, or balancing family responsibilities.

You don't need a six-pack. You don't need perfection. You need energy. You need peace. You need sustainability. Taking care of your body isn't selfish. It's strategic because a healthy body supports a balanced life.

Let's keep building that life; one breath, one bite, one walk at a time.

Personal Reflection Questions:

1. What physical symptoms have you been ignoring that might be your body's way of asking for better care?

2. What false beliefs about health, exercise, or nutrition have you accepted that might be holding you back?

3. How has neglecting your physical health affected your relationships, work performance, or emotional well-being?

4. What small, sustainable change to your daily routine could you realistically maintain to improve your physical wellness?

5. What would your ideal relationship with your body look like one year from now?

Action Steps:

- *Baseline Assessment:* Take honest stock of your current physical health. Note your energy levels, pain points, sleep quality, and areas that need improvement.

- *Movement Integration:* Identify three practical ways to incorporate movement into your existing routine, such as walking meetings, stretching during calls, or family dance parties.

- *Kitchen Reset:* Remove one unhealthy food item from your pantry and replace it with a nutritious alternative. Build on this with one swap each week.

- *Sleep Ritual:* Establish a 20-minute pre-sleep routine that signals your body it's time to rest, incorporating dim lights, no screens, gentle stretching, and reading.

- *Accountability Partner:* Find someone to share your health journey with... whether a walking buddy, a meal-prep partner, or someone to check in with on a weekly basis.

We've tended to your body, that vital vessel that carries you through each day's demands. However, physical wellness, while foundational, is only one piece of the puzzle of wholeness. There's another dimension that many productivity books overlook entirely, one that provides meaning, purpose, and a deeper well of resilience when life's pressures mount.

What sustains you when everything else fails? Where do you find hope when circumstances seem hopeless? These questions lead us to explore the often-neglected spiritual dimension of balance, not as an afterthought, but as an essential cornerstone of sustainable well-being. As important as physical wellness is to our balance, true wholeness cannot be achieved without addressing the deeper needs of our spirit.

CHAPTER 10

Nurturing Your Spirit

Attending religious services weekly has been associated with a 68 percent lower risk of deaths of despair among women and a 33 percent lower risk among men (McLean Hospital, 2024; NPR, 2023).

Spiritual Alignment is Essential

Humans are inherently spiritual beings who require more than just physical and mental care to thrive. We often discuss the importance of balancing managing calendars, setting boundaries, and prioritizing both our physical and mental well-being. However, the truth is that none of it truly works without a grounded spirit. You can have a color-coded planner and a perfectly portioned meal prep, and still feel lost because balance doesn't begin in the schedule. It begins in the soul.

Science Backs Up What Faith Has Always Known

What we've known through faith is now being confirmed by science. Researchers are finding that spirituality is not just something we learn, it is something we're hard-wired for.

Studies from Brigham and Women's Hospital suggest that spiritual connection is rooted in the brain's design. In other words, we're neurologically equipped for spiritual experiences. Additional research has suggested that spirituality may have evolved as a form of survival instinct, helping humans to find meaning and connection even in the face of difficulty.

This may explain why more than 80 percent of people around the world identify as religious or spiritual. It is not just cultural, it's biological. And the benefits go beyond belief.

Addiction and Mental Health

Research from Columbia University found that people who deeply value their spirituality have up to an 80 percent lower risk of addiction to drugs or alcohol. Other studies have shown that regular spiritual practice is linked to improved mental health, more resilient behavior, and healthier daily habits.

Longevity and Well-being

Harvard researchers found that people who regularly attend spiritual gatherings "live longer, have less depression, and use fewer harmful substances" (Harvard T.H. Chan School of Public Health, 2022). Most remarkably, attending religious services weekly has been associated with a 68 percent lower risk of deaths of despair among women and a 33 percent lower risk among men (McLean Hospital, 2024; NPR, 2023).

Brain Changes

Scientists studying "praying nuns, meditating monks, and chanting Sikhs" have observed how spiritual practices change the brain in positive ways (BioLogos, 2023). Perhaps most astonishing, brain scans reveal that while depression can thin certain areas of the brain, spiritual practices like prayer and meditation appear to strengthen them. Over time, these regions may even thicken, supporting improved emotional function and long-term well-being.

When we combine what science tells us with what faith teaches us, we gain a fuller picture of how spirituality enables us to "embrace life with depth" and view our journey as a "cohesive whole" (Schwartz et al., 2021).

As Einstein once said, "Science without religion is lame, religion without science is blind." When faith and science work together, we get a fuller picture... not just of the brain, but of the soul. The question is no longer whether spirituality works. It's how we can root our lives in it more intentionally.

The Foundation of Spiritual Balance

The world teaches us to control, to hustle, and to strive, but faith reminds us that we are not meant to carry this alone (Matthew 11:28).

In my research and personal life, I've seen this over and over: the most resilient people, especially those in high-stress jobs, didn't rely solely on willpower. They leaned on faith, on the quiet strength that comes from knowing they are held by something greater than themselves.

When your spirit is aligned with God:

- Your decisions get clearer (Proverbs 3:5-6)

- Your strength multiplies (Isaiah 40:31)

- Your peace deepens (Philippians 4:6-7)

Faith doesn't erase the storm, but it reminds you who's in the boat with you ;-) These quiet moments of connection complement the mental and physical practices we've explored, completing the foundation for a truly balanced life.

Grounding: Reconnecting with God in a Loud World

In a noisy, fast-paced world, we often lose connection with ourselves, with peace, with God. Grounding brings us back (Psalm 46:10).

Grounding Practices:

- *Breathwork* - Deep breathing helps quiet the mind and body.

- *Nature Walks* - Creation speaks of God's presence. Listen.

- *Gratitude Lists* - Shift your focus from stress to blessings.

- *Stillness* - Silence isn't empty. It's where God speaks.

Even just 5 minutes of presence can reconnect you to a sense of divine peace.

The Power of Prayer and Faith-Based Meditation

Prayer isn't a checklist. It's a conversation. A lifeline. A release. Prayer reminds you:

- You're not alone.

- You're not in control, and that's okay.

- You are seen, heard, and loved.

Biblical meditation is not about emptying your mind; it's about filling it with truth (Psalm 1:2). Use worship music, Scripture, or quiet listening prayer to create space for God. Ways to deepen your practice:

- Start your day with Scripture: Let God speak before the world does.

- Pray throughout the day: Whisper prayers between meetings, errands, or moments of stress.

- End your day in reflection: Give thanks to God. Release your worries. Rest in Him.

Faith in Real Life: Everyday Integration
Spiritual life isn't reserved for Sunday mornings or crisis moments. Let faith lead you through the day, not just to the day. It should show up:

- In how you begin your day.

- In how you respond to conflict.

- In how you carry burdens.

Practical Integration:

- Before email, pray (Proverbs 16:3)

- Before tough conversations, pause and pray (Nehemiah 2:4)

- Before sleep, surrender your day (Psalm 4:8)

Closing Truths to Carry with You
When you nurture your spirit, your peace is no longer hostage to your circumstances (Matthew 6:33). And that, helps to manage the imbalance. With mind, body, and spirit aligned, you're now equipped to implement the practical boundaries and routines we'll develop in the chapters ahead.

- Faith grounds your life when everything else feels out of control.

- Stillness makes space for God's voice to be louder than fear.

- Prayer is power. Not because of your words, but because of who you're speaking to.

- Daily habits matter. Small moments of connection make a big difference.

- Spiritual balance isn't a feeling. It's a practice.

Personal Reflection Questions:

1. When do you feel most connected to something greater than yourself? What elements of that experience could you incorporate more

regularly?

2. What spiritual practices did you once value that have fallen away in the busyness of life?

3. How does your current spiritual health affect how you respond to stress, conflict, or uncertainty?

4. What questions about purpose or meaning keep resurfacing in your life that might be calling for spiritual attention?

5. If your spiritual life were as prioritized as your professional life, what would look different about your daily routine?

Action Steps

- *Morning Spiritual Practice:* Establish a simple 10-minute spiritual practice to begin each day, such as prayer, scripture reading, meditation, or gratitude.

- *Weekly Sabbath Time:* Set aside a specific time each week (even just a few hours) for spiritual rest and renewal, free from the pressure of productivity.

- *Find Spiritual Community:* Identify and reach out to a faith community, study group, or mentor who can support your spiritual growth.

- *Nature Connection:* Schedule time each week to be in nature as a way to reconnect with something larger than yourself.

- *Service Commitment:* Find one way to serve others regularly as an expression of your spiritual values and a way to shift focus beyond yourself.

When you **N**urture your spirit alongside your mind and body, you create the foundation for sustainable balance. This holistic approach will become clearer as we integrate all these elements into your personal method for managing life's demands.

With our foundation firmly established in body, mind, and spirit, let's now turn our attention to how these principles come together to create a life of sustainable balance and meaningful impact.

SECTION IV

From Breakdown to Breakthrough

This is where transformation happens. Get the systems, strategy, and support you need to move forward with clarity, calm, and conviction.

Chapter 11

Establishing Routines & Boundaries

Research shows that setting boundaries can lower stress and improve well-being. Meanwhile, it takes an average of 66 days to form a new habit (Recovery Ways, 2024; Lally et al., 2010).

Preserving Resources

Remember the Conservation of Resources Theory we explored in Chapter 3? The principle that stress occurs when we lose or feel threatened with the loss of valuable resources? This understanding becomes especially crucial as we establish boundaries. Each boundary you set is actually a resource-protection strategy, a conscious decision to safeguard your energy, time, relationships, and peace.

When you say no to an additional commitment, you're not just managing your calendar; you're preserving precious personal resources that can then be directed toward your highest priorities. This perspective shifts boundary-setting from a negative act (saying no) to a positive one (protecting what matters).

Creating Space for What Matters

Boundaries sound great until you have to actually set them. For many of us, saying "no" feels wrong. Like we're letting someone down. In reality, boundaries don't shut people out; they make room for what matters most. Boundaries might feel like restrictions, but they're protection for your peace, time, and health. These protective practices directly address the resource drains we identified earlier in the book, creating space for what truly matters while filtering out what depletes you.

Let's explore how to create boundaries that both protect your well-being and enhance your relationships, because contrary to common belief, clear boundaries actually strengthen connections rather than weaken them. What you're learning here forms the **B** in our IMBALANCE Method...

establishing **B**oundaries that protect your peace and create space for what matters most.

The Duality of Work and Family

This division creates a fragmented experience where you're never fully present in either role. At work, you might worry about home responsibilities; at home, work concerns intrude on family time. The mental and emotional switching costs are enormous, depleting your energy and diminishing your effectiveness in both spheres.

This lends to two lives:

- At work: polished, driven, productive.

- At home: tired, authentic, trying to keep it together.

This constant switching drains us. The goal isn't perfection. It's alignment; merging your roles so you're not fragmented.

They say, "You show someone how much you care by how you spend your time." Entrepreneurs especially understand this. The lines blur quickly. However, research shows that involving your family in your work and sharing the journey can reduce conflict. Balance isn't separation. It's inclusion.

Setting Boundaries: Guardrails for Your Peace

Boundaries are how you protect what matters. They don't require permission, just clarity.

1. Know Your PFP: Parameters for Peace

Your Parameters for Peace serve as your personal constitution, guiding your decisions about boundaries. When you clearly define what disturbs your peace and what enhances it, setting boundaries becomes more intuitive and less guilt-inducing. Start by examining your current commitments through this peace-preserving lens:

- Does this commitment bring peace or stress?

- Am I saying "yes" because I want to or because I feel guilty?

- Does this person drain me or support me?

Anything that consistently disturbs your peace needs to be adjusted or removed.

2. Saying "No" Without Guilt

You don't owe everyone your time. Here's how to decline with grace without the guilt...

For work:

- *"Thanks for thinking of me, but I'm at capacity this week."*

- *"I'd love to help, but I'm prioritizing something else right now."*

For social events:

- *"I'm focusing on family time. Let's find a better moment."*

- *"I appreciate the invite, but I'm unplugging this weekend."*

Saying no to them is often a yes to yourself.

3. When People Push Back

Even with clear communication, some people will struggle to respect your newly established boundaries. This resistance is normal and often reflects their own discomfort with change rather than anything you've done wrong. When faced with pushback, remember that protecting your peace isn't selfish, it's necessary:

- Reiterate your "no" without explaining.

- Distance yourself if respect isn't mutual.

- Remove guilt. You're not being mean, you're being wise.

Digital Boundaries: Mastering Technology Before It Masters You

In our increasingly connected world, technology often blurs the boundaries between work and home without our permission. The constant pings, notifications, and accessibility can make true rest impossible. Digital boundaries are non-negotiable in today's environment, serving as the modern moat around your castle of peace. By intentionally managing your relationship with devices and digital communications, you reclaim not just your time, but your attention... perhaps your most precious resource.

- Technology scheduling (specific times to check email/messages)
- Digital sabbaths (tech-free days or weekends)
- Notification management techniques
- Physical separation from devices during key activities
- Digital minimalism practices
- App/screen time limits and tracking
- Email batching methods
- Team communication protocols

Routines: Structure That Frees You
Boundaries guard your time. Routines help you use it wisely.

Without routines:

- Time leaks into distractions.
- You operate on a reactionary basis instead of with intention.
- Everything feels urgent.

With routines:

- Focus increases
- Family time is protected
- Your well-being has a home

Build a Routine That Works
Effective routines aren't rigid prison schedules; they're thoughtfully designed frameworks that eliminate decision fatigue and create dependable rhythms for your most important priorities.

1. Start with Your Non-Negotiables - Begin by identifying what absolutely must happen daily for you to maintain your wellbeing and fulfill your core responsibilities. These aren't 'nice-to-haves', they're essentials:

- Work commitments that directly impact your livelihood
- Family responsibilities that can't be delegated

- Self-care practices that maintain your physical and mental health
- Spiritual connections that ground your day

2. *Time Block Your Day* - Assign specific hours to your priority categories rather than leaving them to chance. This proactive approach ensures important activities don't get pushed aside by the merely urgent:

- Create defined work periods with clear start and end times
- Schedule family time with the same commitment you give to professional meetings
- Protect personal growth and self-care blocks from encroachment
- Build in transition periods between different types of activities

3. *Build in Buffers* - Life rarely unfolds exactly as planned. Cushioning your schedule with small gaps between activities creates flexibility without derailing your entire day:

- Allow 5-10 minutes between meetings for processing and resetting
- Don't schedule activities back-to-back across different locations
- Create a margin for unexpected delays or opportunities
- Recognize that transitions take real time and energy

4. *Schedule Downtime* - Rest isn't what happens after everything else is done, it's an essential component of sustainable productivity and wellbeing:

- Block regular periods for complete disengagement from responsibilities
- Include both active rejuvenation (hobbies, exercise) and passive rest (quiet time, sleep)
- Protect these periods as vigilantly as you would important work commitments
- Recognize that regular downtime actually increases overall productivity

5. *Stay Consistent* - The power of routines emerges through consistency. While flexibility matters, maintaining core patterns builds momentum and reduces resistance:

- Commit to your key routines for at least 30 days before major adjustments

- Recognize that others will adapt to your consistency over time

- When disruptions occur, return to your routine as quickly as possible

Remember that consistency, not perfection, is the goal

Communicate Clearly, And Early

Even the best boundaries and routines fail without clear communication. When others understand your parameters from the beginning, they're more likely to respect them and less likely to take perceived rejections personally.

At Work:

- Be upfront about your work hours.

- Use an email auto-response after hours.

- Speak up when deadlines are unrealistic.

- For early career professionals, find allies who model healthy boundaries, and don't be afraid to establish these practices early, even when workplace culture suggests otherwise.

With Family and Friends:

- Share your priorities out loud.

- Set "unplugged" time for presence.

- Claim quiet time for yourself without apology.

- Boundaries don't work if you whisper them. Speak to them clearly and consistently.

Final Reminders

Anything that disturbs your mental, emotional, or physical well-being must be addressed or removed. As you implement these boundaries and routines, remember these essential principles to guide your practice:

- *Boundaries protect your energy.* They're not selfish, they're necessary.

- *Routines create order.* You don't rise to the level of your intentions; you fall to the level of your systems.

- *Say no without guilt.* If it costs you your peace, it's too high a price.

- *Start small.* You don't need a perfect system, you need a committed one.

- *Communicate with courage.* Clear expectations reduce confusion and resentment.

Your peace is your responsibility. Let's protect it, on purpose.

Personal Reflection Questions

1. Which areas of your life currently lack clear boundaries? How has this affected your peace and energy?

2. Think of a time when saying "no" actually led to something positive. What did this experience teach you?

3. Which relationship or commitment consistently drains your energy? What boundary could you establish to protect your peace?

Action Steps:

1. Identify your three non-negotiable 'Parameters for Peace' this week. Write them on index cards and place them where you'll see them daily, such as your bathroom mirror, desk, or car dashboard.

Implementation guide:

- Set aside 15 minutes of uninterrupted time.

- For each parameter, write:

  - What specifically disturbs your peace in this area?

  - What boundaries would protect this peace?

  - What concrete actions will you take when this boundary is tested?

  (Example: Parameter: Evening family time | Disturbance: Work emails after 7 pm | Boundary: No checking work communications between

7-9 pm | Action: Set phone to Do Not Disturb with automatic reply)

- Place these parameters where you'll see them daily, such as your bathroom mirror, desk, or car dashboard.

- Set a calendar reminder to review these after 3 days to assess effectiveness.

2. *Practice* saying 'no' using one of the scripts provided. Start by declining a low-stakes request this week, noting how you feel before, during, and after.

3. *Design* a 15-minute evening routine with 3-4 specific activities that help you transition from work to family time. Commit to following this routine for seven consecutive days, tracking your experience in a simple journal.

The boundaries and routines you establish now will form the foundation of a more balanced and intentional life. They create the structure within which meaningful connection, productivity, and rest can flourish.

Now that we've established the importance of setting boundaries and creating routines to protect your peace, let's move from theory to action and explore how to implement these principles in your daily life. While establishing boundaries is crucial, implementing them consistently requires strategic planning and accountability. In the next chapter, we'll explore how to activate these systems with practical implementation steps that turn theory into transformative daily practice.

CHAPTER 12

Putting the Plan in Motion

Only 9 percent of Americans keep their New Year's resolutions long-term, but habits anchored in context and repetition are more likely to stick (Wiseman, 2007; Psychology Today, 2024).

From Knowledge to Action

Everything we've explored, from identifying drains to nurturing your whole self, comes together in the IMBALANCE Method you'll master in Chapter 16. For now, let's focus on the action-oriented elements that create immediate change.

You've read the insights. You've reflected on the struggles. You've nodded at the parts that hit home. Now, it's time to *act*. Because balance doesn't come from knowing what to do, it comes from doing it. One small, consistent choice at a time.

This chapter is about *implementation*, not about being perfect or feeling overwhelmed. It's about taking intentional steps toward the life you're called to live, one that aligns with your values, energy, and brings you peace. This approach transforms the time management principles we explored earlier into concrete daily practices that protect your energy for what matters most.

STEP ONE: GET HONEST WITH YOURSELF

Before you dive into strategies, you need clarity. Awareness is the first act of power.

Self-Assessment Questions:

- Do I feel constantly overwhelmed by work or family obligations?

- Am I sacrificing sleep, self-care, or relationships to keep up?

- Do I struggle with saying "no"?

- Is my mental and physical health on the back burner?
- Do I feel spiritually disconnected or emotionally depleted?

You can't fix what you won't face. Take time to answer these. Circle the ones that sting; that's where the work begins.

STEP TWO: CHOOSE THE RIGHT TOOLS FOR THE JOB

Balance isn't one-size-fits-all. Your solution must fit *your* life. However, these proven strategies can be tailored to suit your needs.

1. Focus on High-Impact Activities - The IMBALANCE Method teaches us that not all activities are created equal. Some work tasks and personal commitments generate meaningful results, while others just fill time without moving you toward your values:

- Identify your most meaningful work and personal activities
- Eliminate busy work that creates stress without real value
- Ask regularly: "What activities align most with my core values?"

When you learn to distinguish between busy work and meaningful work, you free up precious time for what truly matters while still accomplishing what's necessary.

2. Set Boundaries That Stick - Boundaries are not walls to keep others out but fences that define where your responsibilities begin and end. They protect your most valuable resources, time, energy, and peace, from being depleted by lesser priorities:

- Define your work hours, and defend them.
- Create "no-phone" zones at home.
- Say no without apology. Your peace is the priority. The strength of your boundaries directly impacts the quality of your relationships, as they enable you to show up with energy and presence for what matters most to you.

3. *Create a Structured Routine* - Structure provides the framework within which freedom can flourish. Far from being restrictive, well-designed routines eliminate the mental fatigue of constant decision-making and create reliable anchors throughout your day:

- Plan your day the night before.

- Block out time for work, family, rest, and YOU.

- Review weekly and adjust without guilt. By establishing predictable patterns for essential activities, you create mental space for creativity, connection, and the spontaneity that enriches life.

4. *Use the "Big Rocks" Analogy* - Imagine your time as a glass jar you need to fill:

- Big rocks = family, faith, health, and deep work

- Pebbles = errands, emails, minor tasks

- Sand = scrolling, gossip, distractions

If you fill your jar with sand and pebbles first, the big rocks won't fit. But place the big rocks in first, and the pebbles and sand will settle around them. This visual reminds us to schedule our priorities (the big rocks) before attending to less important matters. Otherwise, life's trivialities will consume all your time, leaving no space for what truly matters.

5. *Protect Your Energy* - Your energy, physical, mental, emotional, and spiritual, is the currency with which you purchase your life experiences. How you generate, preserve, and direct this energy will determine the quality of everything you do:

- Sleep isn't optional; it's foundational.

- Move daily, even if just 10 minutes.

- Eat to fuel, not to escape.

- Pray, breathe, and reset. Protecting your energy isn't selfish; it's the prerequisite for serving others effectively and showing up fully in all areas of your life.

6. Use Tech, Don't Let It Use You - Technology should function as a servant, not a master. In today's constantly connected world, intentional tech boundaries are essential for maintaining focus, presence, and mental clarity:

- Set "Do Not Disturb" hours.
- Use tools like Google Calendar or Asana.
- Automate low-priority tasks.
- Check your email at specific times, not constantly. When you control your relationship with technology rather than letting it control you, you reclaim countless hours of attention and reduce the mental fragmentation that inhibits deep work and meaningful connection.

7. Weekly Check-In - Balance isn't static; it's a dynamic process that requires regular adjustment as circumstances and priorities shift. A weekly review practice allows you to course-correct before small imbalances become major problems:

- What gave me energy?
- What drained me?
- What needs to shift?

This reflective practice transforms balance from a distant goal into an ongoing conversation with yourself about what's working, what isn't, and what adjustments will better serve your values and vision.

Here are tools you can implement immediately. Don't get paralyzed by choice or perfectionism. Select one that resonates with you and commit to practicing it consistently. Mastery comes from sustained application, not from collecting techniques. Start where you are, with what feels most relevant to your current challenges, and build from there.

- » Time Management Apps:
  - Trello, Asana – Task tracking
  - Google Calendar – Scheduling with intention

- Pomodoro Timer – Stay focused with breaks

» Mindfulness & Spiritual Care:
  - Headspace, Calm – Guided meditation
  - YouVersion Bible App – Daily devotionals
  - Sleep Cycle App – Improves rest quality

» Productivity & Consistency:
  - Evernote, Notion – Organize ideas and notes
  - Habit Trackers – Build consistency, one step at a time

STEP THREE: MAKE IT PERSONAL

The Work-Life Balance Wheel

Draw a circle. Divide it into 6 parts: work, family, faith, health, personal growth, hobbies. Rate each from 1 to 10. Is the wheel balanced or bumpy? Focus on the lowest scores first.

The "What Can I Let Go?" List

You can't add peace without subtracting pressure:

- Write down all your responsibilities.
- Highlight what's truly essential.
- Cross out what's draining you but adds no value.
- Circle what can be delegated or postponed.

Weekly Reflection Journal

This is where transformation lives; in the reflection. Ask yourself:

- What did I do well this week?
- What needs improvement?
- What will I change next week?

Takeaways

Balance isn't a destination; it's a decision you make daily. Awareness is power. Boundaries are protection. Routines are freedom. Small steps become lasting shifts.

You've done the reading. You've done the reflecting. Now it's time to become. Let's build the life you were made for; one boundary, one breath, one big rock at a time.

Personal Reflection Questions:

1. Which of the strategies mentioned resonates most with you, and why? What resistance do you feel about implementing it?

2. Considering your current schedule, what are the "big rocks" that deserve priority? Which "sand" activities are taking up too much space?

3. If you could change just one habit to improve your work-life balance this month, what would it be?

Action Steps:

- Complete the Work-Life Balance Wheel exercise and identify your lowest-scoring area to prioritize first.

- Select one time management app from the list provided and set it up to track your primary responsibilities.

- Create your "What Can I Let Go?" list and commit to eliminating or delegating at least three items this week.

With our implementation strategies in place, it's time to formalize your commitment to change by setting clear, actionable goals that will transform these insights into lasting habits. Implementation is powerful, but lasting change requires clear targets. Next, we'll explore how to set meaningful goals that align with your deepest values.

CHAPTER 13

Set the Goal, Start the Change

Behavior change is more sustainable when paired with consistent repetition in specific settings (Oxford Research Encyclopedia of Psychology, 2024).

Setting Goals That Transform

You've come a long way. You've explored the imbalance, discovered the root causes, learned how to care for your mind, body, and spirit, and now it's time to put it all into action because knowledge is great. But transformation? That happens when goals become habits and intentions become movement.

Let's map out how to set meaningful goals and stick to them.

IMBALANCE Goals

A goal without a plan is just a wish. The IMBALANCE Method helps you create goals that protect your peace while driving progress. Each letter represents a checkpoint for meaningful goal-setting that aligns with your values and sustains your well-being.

We'll explore the complete IMBALANCE Method in Chapter 16, but for now, focus on creating goals that serve your well-being, not just your productivity.

From Vague to Clear:

- Instead of, *"I want to be healthier,"* try, *"I will walk for 30 minutes, 4 times a week, for the next 3 months."*

- Instead of, *"I want more time with my kids,"* try, *"I will have device-free dinners with my family 5 nights a week."*

Write one goal in each area: work, personal life, health. Start small. Stay consistent. These structured targets transform the boundaries we established earlier into measurable actions that create momentum toward the balanced life you envision.

While having goals is important, the way you structure them determines their effectiveness. Understanding the interplay between short-term and long-term objectives helps create a sustainable approach to change.

Short-Term vs. Long-Term Goals

You need both. Short-term = daily fuel, long-term = life vision. You need both to build lasting change.

- *Short-term goals* - keep you grounded in the present, create quick wins, and motivate you. An example is "Read 15 minutes before bed each night."

- *Long-term goals* - give your life direction. An example is, "Finish my degree within 2 years while raising a family."

This balance appears differently across various life stages. Someone in their twenties might balance career development goals with establishing healthy work patterns, while someone in midlife might focus on family milestones alongside professional achievements. With your goals clearly defined, visualization becomes a powerful tool to reinforce your commitment and program your mind for success.

Visualization: See It Before You Become It

Your brain responds to imagery. Visualizing success activates belief. Try this:

- *Journal*: Write what your life will look like one year from now if you follow through.

- *Vision Board*: Use photos, quotes, Scripture, anything that reminds you of where you're headed.

- *Affirmations*: Speak truth over your future. "I am balancing work and family with peace and grace."

Even the most beautifully visualized goals require consistent tracking to become a reality. What gets measured gets managed, and ultimately accomplished.

Track It or Lose It

You can't grow what you don't measure. Ways for you to track your progress:

- Weekly Check-ins

- Progress Journals

- Scorecards (Rate 1–10 in areas like stress, family time, energy, etc.)

Miss a goal? Don't quit. Adjust. Don't abandon. No matter how disciplined we are, human connection and external accountability dramatically increase our chances of following through on our commitments.

Accountability: Don't Go Alone

You're more likely to keep moving when someone is walking beside you. Find someone who will:

• Challenge you

• Check in weekly

• Celebrate your wins and call out your excuses

Choose one person to walk with you for the next 30 days. Text them now. In our digital age, technology can either distract us from our goals or accelerate our progress toward them. The difference lies in how intentionally we select and use our digital tools.

Final Coaching Takeaways

You're not here to *try*. You're here to *change*.

• You don't need a perfect goal. You need a clear one.

• Short wins build long victories.

• Visualization builds belief.

• Tracking builds accountability.

• Consistency builds transformation.

One Final Challenge

Balance doesn't happen overnight. It happens when ordinary people take consistent action in pursuit of an extraordinary life. Right now, write down ONE goal.

- Make it specific and measurable.

- Ensure it aligns with your values.

- Set a reminder to check in once a week.

- Tell someone about it.

- Start today!

Personal Reflection Questions:

1. What vague intentions about work-life balance have you been carrying without turning them into specific goals?

2. Which area of your life would benefit most from a clear, achievable goal right now?

3. How might setting intentional goals help you overcome the barriers you face in creating better balance?

Action Steps:

1. Create one specific goal for each area: work, personal life, and health. Post them where you'll see them daily.

Milestone markers:

- Week 1: Goals written and posted where you'll see them daily

- Week 2: First obstacle encountered and strategy adjusted

- Week 3: Small win identified and celebrated in at least one area

- Week 4: Progress measured and goals refined based on what you've learned

Say for example you set a health goal to walk 30 minutes, 4 times a week, for the next 3 months.

- Week 1 milestone: Walking schedule established and first two walks completed

- Week 2 milestone: Weather obstacle identified; indoor alternative created

- Week 3 milestone: Completed all 4 walks; noticed improved sleep quality

- Week 4 milestone: 3 of 4 walks completed; adjusted timing to morning for better consistency

2. Select an accountability partner and schedule a specific check-in time for next week.

3. Choose one tracking tool (journal, app, or scorecard) and commit to using it for the next 21 days.

While setting goals is essential, seeing how others have successfully navigated similar challenges can provide both inspiration and practical wisdom. Sometimes the most powerful motivation comes from witnessing real transformation in action, which is precisely what we'll explore next.

CHAPTER 14

Case Studies & Success Stories

Social support significantly improves habit formation and behavior change success over time (Quenza, 2024; Oxford Research Encyclopedia of Psychology, 2024).

I recall feeling like an imposter when discussing work-life balance, teaching principles I struggled to apply in my own life. Balance isn't about flawless execution; it's about honest effort and continual adjustment. These stories aren't just inspiration; they're proof that the principles in this book aren't theoretical ideals but practical paths walked by real people just like you and me.

Work-life balance isn't just a theory or a catchy phrase. It's a journey; one real people navigate every single day, not perfectly, but intentionally. These stories bring to life the principles explored throughout this book, illustrating how real people have applied these concepts to transform their experiences of both work and home.

BTB: Eight Journeys to Balance

In this chapter, we will examine eight stories of individuals who faced burnout, overwhelm, and guilt, and made bold yet straightforward decisions to reclaim their time, energy, and relationships. These composite narratives are derived from real people with real struggles seeking real change. Let them inspire you. More importantly, let them remind you that balance is possible for you, too.

The Executive's Breakthrough

I was a high-powered executive who spent most of my week at the office, chasing numbers while missing milestones at home. For years, I told myself, "I'm doing this for them." But one night, my daughter said, "You're never here." That broke me.

What changed my life was setting boundaries that actually stuck. I created a hard stop at 6 PM, no more late nights. Family came first. I instituted tech-free dinners, focusing on conversation rather than notifications. Most importantly, I finally trusted my team and stepped back from micromanaging.

My company still thrived. My marriage and relationship with my kids improved immeasurably. I redefined what success meant to me: being present, not just productive.

> » *BALANCE LESSON: Your family doesn't want your title; they want your time.*

The Single Parent's Revelation

As a nurse and single parent, I often felt like I was always behind at work, at home, and in my own thoughts. I was stretched thin and emotionally drained. The guilt never let up. Until I realized something had to change.

I started time-blocking for family just as deliberately as I scheduled my shifts. I carved out 5 minutes each morning for prayer and gratitude, a small moment of stillness to reset my spirit. Most significantly, I finally asked for help, leaning on friends, coworkers, and family members who had always offered support that my pride had prevented me from accepting.

My guilt was gradually replaced with presence. My mood stabilized. My clarity returned. I stopped trying to do it all and instead, I embraced doing what mattered most.

> » *BALANCE LESSON: You don't have to do it alone. Let people show up for you.*

The Entrepreneur's Integration

Running a growing business consumed everything in my life. My spouse felt like an afterthought, and my children barely knew what I did all day. So I stopped trying to separate my life and started integrating it instead.

I brought my family into appropriate aspects of the business, my spouse helped with the books, and my oldest child contributed ideas for marketing. I declared weekends sacred space, completely disconnected from work demands. Instead of saving up for one big annual vacation, I planned small, meaningful getaways throughout the year.

The result? My family became an integral part of my mission, not a competitor for my attention. My marriage deepened through shared purpose. And surprisingly, my business continued to grow, but so did my joy, because success finally included the people who mattered most.

> » BALANCE LESSON: *You don't always need a balance between work and home. Sometimes, you need a connection between them.*

The Retail Solution

Working nights and weekends in retail meant missing family gatherings and living on an opposite schedule from everyone else. The constant rotation between morning and evening shifts made any kind of routine nearly impossible. The breakthrough came when I stopped trying to force a fixed plan and began using a flexible strategy I call "micro-scheduling."

Instead of setting a standard routine, I created three types of days, each with a few core habits that could adjust to whatever shift I was working. No matter what time I started or ended work, I committed to three things: 20 minutes of movement, 10 minutes of intentional connection with someone I love (even if it was just a phone call), and five minutes of journaling or reflection.

This gave me a sense of control and rhythm in the midst of constant change. It also helped my family understand that my energy wasn't personal… it was just affected by the job. Communication improved, and so did my resilience.

> » BALANCE LESSON: *You don't need a perfect routine to create stability. When your schedule is unpredictable, build consistency through habits that can flex with your day.*

From Knowledge to Action

I spent years collecting wisdom about work-life balance… books, podcasts, and workshops… until the break room at the store where I manage was lined with solutions. Yet between opening shifts, weekend work, and seasonal rushes in retail, my life remained chaotic.

The turning point came during a rare Sunday off when my seven-year-old daughter asked, "Are you actually going to play with me, or just check the store inventory on your phone the whole time?" Her words cut deep because they were true.

That day I realized that knowledge without action is just decoration. The path to change, especially with unpredictable retail hours, isn't found in more information, it's in the small, consistent steps we take every single day.

> » BALANCE LESSON: *Wisdom means nothing without action. The smallest steps forward count more than the biggest plans never started.*

Rideshare Balance

Driving for a rideshare company while pursuing a creative passion brought a lot of flexibility, but it also came with unpredictable income, irregular hours, and constant pressure to accept every ride. It felt like the algorithm was in charge of my life, not me.

The shift happened when I started using financial benchmarks instead of time limits. I set clear earnings goals for each part of the day. Once I met my morning target, I stopped working; no matter how tempting it was to keep going. I also blocked off two full days each week just for my music and my family. Those days were non-negotiable.

Sometimes I made a little less money, but the energy, clarity, and creative focus I regained more than made up for it. I became more productive and more present, both in my work and in my life.

> » BALANCE LESSON: *Boundaries can work even when your schedule doesn't. Defining success by intention instead of hours can protect your energy and fuel your purpose*

The Someday Shift

"Someday I'll have more balance" was my mantra for years, until a health scare forced me to confront the cost of perpetual postponement. Lying in that hospital bed, I realized 'someday' is a dangerous word. It permits us to delay the very changes our hearts are desperate for.

That day, I stopped waiting for the perfect time to create balance and started setting concrete goals that would move me toward it, even if they were small at first. Looking back, that shift from someday to today wasn't just about time management; it was about reclaiming my life.

> » BALANCE LESSON: *Waiting for the right time delays the right life. Progress begins with the choice to act now.*

The Young Professional's Balance

Fresh out of college and working in tech, I quickly found myself trapped in a cycle of constant availability, impostor syndrome, and burnout. My friends were experiencing the same thing, but we all thought this was 'paying our dues' and necessary for success.

The breaking point came when I realized I had canceled plans with friends six weekends in a row for 'urgent' work that somehow always arose on Friday afternoons. My health was suffering, my relationships were fading, and despite all the hours, my productivity was declining.

I started by creating two separate phone profiles: one for work and one for personal use. Then I began setting expectations with my team about response times. Instead of trying to prove myself by being available 24/7, I focused on the quality of my work during regular hours.

The most crucial step was finding a mentor who modeled healthy boundaries while still advancing in their career. Seeing someone successful who didn't sacrifice everything else permitted me to create balance for myself.

My performance reviews improved, I reconnected with my support network, and I developed a sustainable approach to my career that didn't require burning out every few months.

> » BALANCE LESSON: *Early intervention prevents deeper burnout. The habits you establish in your early career will shape your relationship with work for decades to come.*

How to Apply These Lessons to Your Life

All eight individuals made different choices, but shared the same realization. Balance isn't found through perfect time management or productivity hacks. It's created when your priorities align with your values, when your present focus matches what truly matters, and when the people you love feel the weight of your presence, not just your provision.

These people didn't overhaul their entire lives overnight. They made small, consistent changes that created big, lasting results. You can do the same.

Start here:

- Set a hard stop for work.
- Block out family time, and protect it.

- Ask for help, and receive it.

- Look for ways to merge your life, not just separate it.

- Focus on what matters most, not just what's loudest.

Balance doesn't mean doing it all perfectly. It means doing the right things on purpose. Let these stories encourage you, but don't compare. Your journey is yours. Your rhythm, your priorities, your peace. All that matters is that you start.

What is one small shift you can make today to restore balance in your life? Write it down. Say it out loud. Start it now. Because the life you want? You're not far from it, you're just one decision away.

Personal Reflection Questions:

1. Which of these three stories resonates most deeply with your current situation? Why?

2. What specific strategy from these case studies could you implement immediately in your own life?

3. What's your biggest excuse for not making changes toward better balance, and how do these stories challenge that excuse?

Action Steps:

- Identify the case study that most closely matches your situation and adopt one specific strategy that the case study used.

- Write down your own "success story" as if you're looking back one year from now. What specific changes did you make?

- Share your intended changes with someone close to you who will both support and hold you accountable.

- Having witnessed the transformative power of these principles in action through real-life stories, let's bring everything together and chart your path forward toward a more balanced, purposeful life.

While these stories demonstrate the transformative power of intentional change, they all share one common thread: each person moved from understanding their challenges to creating a comprehensive framework for addressing them.

CHAPTER 15
The Next Step Forward

New habits are most likely to take root during life transitions when people are open to change and willing to disrupt old routines (ScienceDirect, 2018; Positive Psychology, 2021).

The Ongoing Journey to Balance

Let's be clear, you didn't just read a book. You made a commitment to grow. To reflect. To change. You paused long enough to say: *Something in my life isn't working, and I'm ready to do something about it.*

That's powerful. And it deserves to be celebrated.

Throughout our journey from understanding burnout to implementing solutions, you've built a foundation for sustainable change, not just managing imbalance but transforming your relationship with it. So, in this chapter, we'll summarize what you've learned, and more importantly, we'll help you prepare for *what's next.*

Key Takeaways from This Journey

1. Balance Isn't a Destination, It's a Practice

- You won't always feel balanced, but you *can* live in alignment.

- Life will shift. Priorities will compete. What matters is that you continue to adjust with grace and awareness.

- Don't chase perfection. Chase presence.

2. Boundaries & Routines Protect Your Peace

- No one will guard your time like you can.

- Learn to say no, without apology.

- Build routines that support the life you say you want.

3. Health Is Your Foundation

- Your physical, mental, and spiritual health must be non-negotiable.
- Sleep is sacred. Movement is medicine. Mindfulness is maintenance.
- When you feel good, you lead better. Love better. Live better.

4. Relationships Are the Real Wealth

- You show love by how you spend your time.
- The people closest to you should get the best of you, not just what's left of you.
- Invest deeply in those who nourish you. Release what drains you.

5. Goals Create Momentum

- Use the IMBALANCE Method for goal-setting that protects your peace
- Consistency > motivation.
- Track your progress, reflect weekly, and hold yourself accountable.

The Power of Habits

> *"You do not rise to the level of your goals. You fall to the level of your systems." - James Clear*

Success isn't built on motivation; it's built on habits. Start small. Stay consistent. Build routines that reinforce who you're becoming. This comprehensive approach, caring for your mind, body, and spirit while establishing practical boundaries, creates not just momentary relief but lasting resilience in the face of life's inevitable pressures.

- *Identity-based habits:* Don't just say, "I want to eat healthy." Say, "I'm someone who prioritizes wellness."
- *Track what matters:* What gets measured improves.
- *Design your environment for success:* Eliminate distractions. Set up reminders. Surround yourself with support.

Communities to Keep You Grounded:

- Find a life or balance coach.

- Join online groups focused on faith, wellness, or productivity.

- Connect with accountability partners and peer support networks.

Call to Action

This book was never meant to inspire you alone. It was meant to mobilize you. Here's how to begin:

- *Reflect:* What is one small change you can make today to support balance?

- *Decide:* What habit will you commit to for the next 30 days?

- *Share:* Who will hold you accountable?

Write these down. Say them out loud. Take the first step today.

Personal Reflection Questions:

1. Looking back at where you were when you started this book, what's the most significant insight you've gained?

2. What one habit or practice discussed in these chapters could become your cornerstone for lasting change?

3. A year from now, what would "success" in work-life balance look like for you specifically?

Action Steps:

- Schedule a monthly "balance check-in" with yourself for the next six months (put actual dates in your calendar).

- Select three key practices from this book and create visible reminders of them in your workspace and home.

- Write a letter to your future self about the balanced life you're committed to creating, and set a date to read it six months from now.

Throughout this journey, you've gained insights, tools, and inspiration. Now it's time to weave everything together into a cohesive method you can rely on daily. The scattered pieces of wisdom you've collected are about to become a unified framework that will serve as your compass through any season of life.

CHAPTER 16
THE IMBALANCE™
METHOD

You've made it to the final chapter, but this isn't the end; it's your beginning. Everything you've learned, every insight you've gained, every moment of recognition comes together here in one powerful framework you can use for the rest of your life.

The irony isn't lost on me: using the word "imbalance" to create balance. That's exactly the point. Perfect balance doesn't exist. What exists is the intentional management of imbalance, and that's what this method gives you: a roadmap for navigating life's inevitable seasons of competing demands.

This isn't just another acronym to memorize. This is your daily compass, your weekly check-in, your monthly reset. When life feels overwhelming, when priorities compete, when you've lost your way, come back here. Let this method guide you home to what matters most.

This is an overview of the IMBALANCE Method. For detailed implementation strategies, daily practices, and step-by-step guides, refer to *Appendix D: The IMBALANCE Method Daily Implementation Guide.*

THE IMBALANCE METHOD
Nine Steps from Burnout to Breakthrough

I - IDENTIFY what's draining you

- *"You can't manage what you don't understand"*

- *The Foundation:* Before you can protect your resources, you must know what's depleting them. This isn't about blame; it's about awareness.

- *Key Practices:*
  1. Track your energy levels for one week to identify patterns
  2. Recognize warning signs before burnout takes hold
  3. Name the invisible burdens: perfectionism, people-pleasing, comparison
  4. Complete your Personal Resources Inventory monthly (*Appendix A*)

- *Quick Check:* Can you name your top 3 energy drains right now?

M - **MIND** body, spirit nurturing

- *"Burnout recovery starts from the inside out"*

- *The Foundation:* You are not just a productivity machine. You're a whole person with mental, physical, and spiritual needs that must be met for sustainable success.

- *Key Practices:*
  1. *Mind* - Daily mindfulness, reframe negative thoughts, practice forgiveness
  2. *Body* - Prioritize sleep, move daily, eat to fuel your purpose
  3. *Spirit* - Connect with deeper purpose, spend time in nature, engage with faith

- *Quick Check:* Which of these three areas (mind, body, or spirit) feels most neglected right now?

B - **BOUNDARIES** that protect your peace

- *"Boundaries don't shut people out; they make room for what matters most"*

- *The Foundation:* Your peace is not negotiable. Boundaries are the guardrails that protect your energy, time, and emotional well-being from being consumed by lesser priorities.

- *Key Practices:*
    1. Establish your Parameters for Peace (PFP)
    2. Practice saying "no" without guilt or over-explanation
    3. Communicate your boundaries clearly and consistently
    4. Create digital boundaries with specific times for checking devices

- *Quick Check:* What boundary do you most need to establish or strengthen this week?

A - ALIGN your priorities with your values

- *"Your calendar reveals your true priorities"*

- *The Foundation:* The gap between what you say matters and how you spend your time creates internal tension and external chaos. Alignment brings peace.

- *Key Practices:*
    1. Compare your stated values to your actual time investment
    2. Make decisions based on alignment, not just opportunity
    3. Connect your daily work to your deeper "why"
    4. Regularly assess: "Does this move me toward who I want to become?"

- *Quick Check:* If someone looked at your calendar, would they accurately guess your stated priorities?

L - LET GO of what doesn't serve you

- *"You can't add peace without subtracting pressure"*

- *The Foundation:* Your mental and emotional energy are finite. Holding onto what doesn't serve you prevents you from fully embracing what does.

- *Key Practices:*
    1. Release perfectionism, comparison, and past mistakes
    2. Let go of others' expectations and tasks others can do
    3. Practice conscious decision-making about what to release
    4. Replace what you release with something life-giving

- *Quick Check:* What one thing could you let go of this week that would immediately reduce your stress?

A - ACTION through systems that work...

- *"You don't rise to the level of your goals; you fall to the level of your systems"*

- *The Foundation:* Good intentions without systems fail. Sustainable change requires structures that support your desired outcomes, especially when motivation wanes.

- *Key Practices:*
    1. Implement time blocking and the "Big Rocks" analogy
    2. Create weekly planning and daily routine anchors
    3. Establish accountability partnerships

- *Quick Check:* What one system would most transform your daily experience if implemented consistently?

N - NUTURE relationships that matter...

- *"Your work matters, but your people matter more"*

- *The Foundation:* At the end of your life, you won't remember the extra hours you worked, but you'll remember the moments you were fully present with people you love.

- *Key Practices:*
    1. Prioritize presence over productivity in relationships

2. Listen to understand, not just to respond

3. Express specific appreciation regularly

4. Create rituals that strengthen connection

- *Quick Check:* Which relationship needs more intentional investment this week?

C - **CONSISTENCY** over perfection...

- *"Small steps become lasting shifts"*

- *The Foundation:* Perfection is the enemy of progress. Sustainable change comes from small, consistent actions that compound over time, not dramatic overhauls that burn out quickly.

- *Key Practices:*
    1. Start with habits so small you can't fail
    2. Link new behaviors to existing routines
    3. Track progress simply without perfectionism
    4. Plan for setbacks and restart without guilt

- *Quick Check:* What small, consistent action could you maintain daily that would compound into significant change?

E - **EVALUATE** and adjust regularly...

- *"Balance isn't static; it's dynamic"*

- *The Foundation:* Life changes constantly. What worked last season might not work this season. Regular evaluation keeps you aligned with reality and responsive to change.

- *Key Practices:*
    1. Conduct weekly 10-minute evaluations every Sunday
    2. Complete monthly 30-minute assessments

3. Schedule quarterly 2-hour resets for deeper reflection

4. Adjust systems and boundaries based on what you learn

- *Quick Check:* When will you schedule your first weekly evaluation?

STARTING YOUR IMBALANCE JOURNEY

The IMBALANCE framework isn't about perfect execution; it's about intentional navigation. Some days you'll need to focus more on boundaries. Others will require letting go. Some seasons will emphasize nurturing relationships, while others will demand systems and action.

This method meets you where you are and grows with you where you're going.

Your First Steps:

- *Choose ONE letter* from IMBALANCE that resonates most strongly right now

- *Implement one small practice* from that section this week

- *Refer to Appendix D* for detailed daily practices and implementation guides

- *Schedule your first weekly evaluation* in your calendar right now

You don't need to wait until you have it all figured out. You don't need perfect circumstances or unlimited time. You just need to begin.

Start today. Start small. Start now. Because the balanced life you've been longing for isn't a destination you arrive at someday. It's a way of traveling that begins with your very next choice.

The IMBALANCE Method is your compass for the journey. Trust it. Use it. Let it guide you home to what matters most. Welcome to your breakthrough.

Personal Reflection Questions:

1. Which letter of the IMBALANCE Method resonates most strongly with your current situation?

2. What would change in your life if you consistently applied this method for the next 90 days?

3. Who in your life would benefit from seeing you live more aligned with these principles?

Action Steps:

*   *Today:* Choose one letter from IMBALANCE and implement one small practice from that section.

*   *This Week:* Review *Appendix D* and select your daily practices.

*   *This Month:* Work through each letter systematically, adding one new element each week.

*   *Ongoing:* Use the evaluation templates in *Appendix D* for regular check-ins.

The method is complete. Your transformation begins now!

Final Words

Balance is not something you find. It's something you create. You are the architect of your life. You don't need permission to rest. You don't need validation to protect your peace. You don't need perfection to begin again tomorrow.

Choose presence. Choose alignment. Choose peace. Because your time, your family, your dreams, and your health… they're worth fighting for.

As we reach the end of our journey together, remember that balance isn't a destination; it's a continuous practice of intentional choices. The path won't always be straight, and there will be days when equilibrium feels impossible. With each mindful decision, each boundary set, each relationship nurtured, and each moment of self-compassion, you're building something beautiful and sustainable.

The silent struggles we named in Section I now have solutions. The identity questions we explored in Section II now have clarity. The healing work we undertook in Section III has created a foundation. The practical systems we've developed in Section IV provide the framework for sustainable change.

Your balanced life may not look like anyone else's, and that's exactly as it should be. Take what you've learned here, make it your own, and step forward with confidence. The world needs your wisdom, your energy, and your presence, not what's left of you, but the very best of you. Life will always bring new imbalances to manage, but now you have the tools to meet them with grace, purpose, and clarity. Now go live that balanced life you were created for!

REFERENCES LIST

American Psychological Association. (2023). Work in America Survey: Workplaces as engines of psychological health and wellbeing. https://www.apa.org/pubs/reports/work-in-america/2023-workplace-health-well-being

Centers for Disease Control and Prevention. (2024). Benefits of physical activity. https://www.cdc.gov/physical-activity-basics/benefits/index.html

Gallup. (2015). Americans' perceived time crunch no worse than past. https://news.gallup.com/poll/187982/americans-perceived-time-crunch-no-worse-past.aspx

Gallup. (2023). Time pressures, stress common for Americans. https://news.gallup.com/poll/103456/time-pressures-stress-common-americans.aspx

Goh, J., Pfeffer, J., & Zenios, S. A. (2016). The relationship between workplace stressors and mortality and health costs in the United States. Management Science, 62(2), 608–628. https://doi.org/10.1287/mnsc.2014.2115

Great Place to Work & Maven. (2020). 9.8 million working mothers in the U.S. are suffering from burnout. CNBC. https://www.cnbc.com/2020/12/03/millions-of-working-mothers-in-the-us-are-suffering-from-burnout.html

McKinsey & Company. (2019). How dual-career couples find fulfillment at work. https://www.mckinsey.com/capabilities/people-and-organizational-performance/our-insights/how-dual-career-couples-find-fulfillment-at-work

McLean Hospital. (2024). Understanding spirituality and mental health. https://www.mcleanhospital.org/essential/spirituality

National Alliance on Mental Illness. (2024). The 2024 NAMI Workplace Mental Health Poll. https://www.nami.org/support-education/publications-reports/survey-reports/the-2024-nami-workplace-mental-health-poll/

National Center for Complementary and Integrative Health. (2023). Meditation and mindfulness: Effectiveness and safety. https://www.nccih.nih.gov/health/meditation-and-mindfulness-effectiveness-and-safety

National Institutes of Health. (2024). Women may realize health benefits of regular exercise more than men. https://www.nih.gov/news-events/news-releases/women-may-realize-health-benefits-regular-exercise-more-men

Occupational Safety and Health Administration. (n.d.). Workplace Stress. https://www.osha.gov/workplace-stress

Oxford Research Encyclopedia of Psychology. (2024). Habit formation and behavior change. https://oxfordre.com/psychology/display/10.1093/acrefore/9780190236557.001.0001/acrefore-9780190236557-e-129

Positive Psychology. (2021). How are habits formed? The psychology of habit formation. https://positivepsychology.com/how-habits-are-formed/

Psychology Today. (2024). Habit formation. https://www.psychologytoday.com/us/basics/habit-formation

Quenza. (2024). Charting a path to transformation: The science behind behavior change planning. https://quenza.com/blog/behavior-change-planning/

Recovery Ways. (2024). Setting healthy boundaries: A key to improving mental health. https://www.recoveryways.com/rehab-blog/setting-healthy-boundaries

Appendix A: Personal Resources Inventory

INSTRUCTIONS - Rate your current level for each resource type on a scale of 1-10, with 1 being "critically depleted" and 10 being "abundantly full."

PHYSICAL RESOURCES:

- Energy level: ___/10
- Sleep quality: ___/10
- Physical health: ___/10
- Nutrition: ___/10

MENTAL RESOURCES:

- Focus capability: ___/10
- Decision-making clarity: ___/10
- Creativity: ___/10
- Learning capacity: ___/10

EMOTIONAL RESOURCES:

- Emotional regulation: ___/10
- Stress resilience: ___/10
- Relationship energy: ___/10
- Joy/positive emotion: ___/10

SPIRITUAL RESOURCES:

- Sense of purpose: ___/10
- Connection to values: ___/10
- Perspective on challenges: ___/10
- Faith/hope/meaning: ___/10

REFLECTION QUESTIONS:

1. Which resource areas are most depleted right now?

2. What specific activities or practices reliably replenish these resources for you?

3. What is currently depleting your resources the fastest?

4. What one change could you make this week to better protect your most depleted resource?

RESOURCE REPLENISHMENT PLAN:

- One daily practice: _____

- One weekly practice: _____

- One monthly practice: _____

TOTAL SCORE INTERPRETATION:

- 120-160 points: ***THRIVING*** - You have strong resource reserves across all areas. Focus on maintaining these practices and being a resource for others.

- 90-119 points: ***BUILDING*** - You're developing good resource management. Identify your lowest-scoring areas for targeted improvement.

- 60-89 points: ***RECOVERING*** - Significant resource depletion requiring intentional replenishment. Prioritize 1-2 areas for immediate attention.

- Below 60 points: ***CRITICAL*** - Severe resource depletion. Consider professional support alongside implementing gentle, sustainable changes.

WHAT YOUR SCORES MEAN:

- Scores of 7+ in any area indicate strength to build upon
- Scores of 4-6 suggest areas needing consistent attention
- Scores of 1-3 require immediate, focused intervention

NEXT STEPS BASED ON YOUR RESULTS:

1. Identify your lowest-scoring category - This becomes your primary focus

2. Choose ONE specific practice from that category to implement this week

3. Set a realistic target - Aim to improve your lowest score by 2 points in 30 days

4. Reassess monthly to track progress and adjust strategies

APPENDIX B: IMPLEMENTATION ROADMAP

30-Day Balance Breakthrough Plan

Week 1: Assessment & Awareness

Day 1-2: Complete Balance Wheel assessment

Day 3-4: Track energy levels and identify drains

Day 5-6: Catalog current boundaries (or lack thereof)

Day 7: Reflect and identify top 3 priority areas for change

Week 2: Foundation Building

Day 8-9: Establish morning routine with mindfulness practice

Day 10-11: Set up environment for success (physical spaces)

Day 12-13: Create time blocks for priorities in calendar

Day 14: Select and set up tracking system for habits

Week 3: Boundaries & Implementation

Day 15-16: Craft and communicate key boundaries

Day 17-18: Implement technology management plan

Day 19-20: Practice saying "no" to one low-priority request

Day 21: Review progress and adjust as needed

Week 4: Integration & Support

Day 22-23: Connect with accountability partner

Day 24-25: Integrate physical activity and nutrition plan

Day 26-27: Establish evening wind-down routine

Day 28-30: Reflect, celebrate wins, and set next 30-day goals

Appendix C: Balance Metrics Self-Assessment Tool

Balance Breakthrough Self-Assessment
Rate each area from 1-10 before beginning your journey and reassess monthly

Physical Wellbeing

Energy level throughout day: ___/10

Quality of sleep: ___/10

Consistency of physical activity: ___/10

Nutritional choices: ___/10

Mental & Emotional Health

Ability to focus: ___/10

Mental clarity: ___/10

Emotional regulation: ___/10

Stress management: ___/10

Relationships

Quality of family connections: ___/10

Presence during interactions: ___/10

Communication effectiveness: ___/10

Boundary maintenance: ___/10

Work Effectiveness

Productivity during work hours: ___/10

Ability to prioritize: ___/10

Satisfaction with output: ___/10

Work-home separation: ___/10

Spiritual Connection

Sense of purpose: ___/10

Connection to values: ___/10

Time for reflection: ___/10

Peace and contentment: ___/10

Scoring Guide:

40 or below in any category: Critical attention needed

41-69: Improvement opportunity

70-89: Building strength

90+: Thriving (maintain practices)

APPENDIX D: THE IMBALANCE™ METHOD

Implementation Guide

This appendix provides detailed implementation strategies, daily practices, and step-by-step guides for applying the IMBALANCE Method in your everyday life. Use this as your practical reference guide.

DAILY IMPLEMENTATION PRACTICES

Morning Compass (2 minutes) - As you start your day, briefly consider:

- **I**: What might drain me today, and how can I protect against it?
- **M**: How will I nurture my mind, body, or spirit today?
- **B**: What boundary do I need to maintain today?

Evening Reflection (3 minutes) - Before you end your day, ask:

- **A**: Did my actions align with my priorities today?
- **L**: What can I let go of from today?
- **A**: What action served me well today that I want to repeat?
- **N**: How did I nurture my key relationships today?
- **C**: What small consistent action did I maintain today?
- **E**: What needs adjustment for tomorrow?

When You Feel Overwhelmed (1 minute) - Ask yourself, *"Which do I most need right now?"*

- Feeling scattered? **IDENTIFY** what's draining you.
- Feeling depleted? **MANAGE** your mind, body, or spirit.
- Feeling invaded? **ESTABLISH** a boundary.
- Feeling conflicted? **ALIGN** with your values.
- Feeling burdened? **LET GO** of what doesn't serve you.
- Feeling stuck? Take one small **ACTION**.

- Feeling disconnected? **NURTURE** a relationship.

- Feeling discouraged? Focus on **CONSISTENCY**, not perfection.

- Feeling lost? **EVALUATE** and adjust your approach.

DETAILED PRACTICE FRAMEWORKS

The Alignment Audit - Complete this monthly to ensure your time matches your values:

- What do you say matters most in your life?

- Where did you spend the majority of your time last week?

- What's the gap between #1 and #2?

- What one change would better align your time with your values?

The Release Process - Use this when you need to let go of what doesn't serve you:

- *Identify:* What are you holding onto that weighs you down?

- *Acknowledge:* Name why it's been hard to let go

- *Choose:* Make a conscious decision to release it

- *Replace:* Fill that space with something life-giving

The Connection Audit - Assess your key relationships quarterly:

- Who are the 5 most important people in your life?

- When did you last have meaningful, uninterrupted time with each one?

- What would each person say about how present you are when you're together?

- Which relationship needs immediate attention?

Building Consistency Strategies

- *Start Smaller:* If you can't do it for 2 minutes, it's too big to start

- *Link to Existing Habits:* Attach new behaviors to established routines

- *Track Simply:* Use a basic habit tracker or calendar marks
- *Plan for Setbacks:* When you miss a day, restart the next day without guilt

HELPFUL REFERENCE TOOLS

Boundary Scripts That Work

- *"I'd love to help, but I'm at capacity right now."*
- *"That doesn't work for my schedule, but thanks for thinking of me."*
- *"I keep work and family time separate, so I'll respond tomorrow morning."*
- *"I appreciate the invitation, but I'm prioritizing family time this weekend."*
- *"I'm not available for calls after 7 PM, but I can discuss this first thing tomorrow."*

The 1% Rule for Consistency

- Getting 1% better each day results in being 37 times better in a year
- Getting 1% worse each day results in declining to nearly zero
- Small choices compound into life-changing results
- Focus on tiny improvements rather than dramatic changes

EVALUATION TEMPLATES

Weekly Evaluation (10 minutes every Sunday)

What gave me energy this week?

What drained me?

Where did I feel most aligned with my values?

What needs to shift next week?

Which letter of IMBALANCE do I most need to focus on?

Monthly Assessment (30 minutes first Sunday of the month)

- Review your Balance Metrics Assessment (*Appendix C*)
- Celebrate progress in any area that improved
- Identify the one area needing the most attention
- Adjust systems and boundaries based on what you've learned
- Complete The Alignment Audit
- Update your Parameters for Peace if needed

Quarterly Reset (2 hours every 3 months)

- Complete full Personal Resources Inventory (*Appendix A*)
- Reassess your values and priorities; have they shifted?
- Review your boundaries; are they still serving you?
- Complete The Connection Audit for key relationships
- Plan for the upcoming season's unique challenges and opportunities
- Celebrate wins and acknowledge growth areas

IMPLEMENTATION TIMELINE

This Week - Choose ONE letter from IMBALANCE that resonates most strongly right now. Focus only on that one aspect for 7 days. Notice what changes:

- Day 1-2: Implement the practice
- Day 3-4: Notice what's working and what needs adjustment
- Day 5-6: Refine your approach
- Day 7: Evaluate and prepare to add the next element

This Month - Add one new letter each week until you're incorporating all nine elements. Don't try to perfect each one; just begin practicing each element:

- Week 1: Focus on your chosen starting letter
- Week 2: Add a second letter while maintaining the first

- Week 3: Add a third letter, creating a sustainable rhythm
- Week 4: Complete monthly assessment and plan for next month

This Quarter - Use the method as your decision-making filter. When faced with opportunities, commitments, or challenges, ask: "How does this align with my IMBALANCE method?":

- Month 1: Establish daily practices
- Month 2: Integrate weekly evaluations and monthly assessments
- Month 3: Complete first quarterly reset and plan for next quarter

This Year - Let the method evolve with you. As your life changes, your application of these principles will change too. That's not failure; that's wisdom:

- Quarters 1-2: Master the basics and establish sustainable rhythms
- Quarters 3-4: Refine and adapt based on what you've learned

TROUBLESHOOTING COMMON CHALLENGES

"I don't have time for daily practices"

- Start with just the 1-minute overwhelm check
- Use transition times (commuting, waiting) for quick reflections
- Link practices to existing habits (morning coffee, bedtime routine)

"I keep forgetting to do the practices"

- Set phone reminders for morning and evening practices
- Put visual cues in places you'll see them
- Find an accountability partner to check in weekly

"I feel guilty setting boundaries"

- Remember: boundaries protect your ability to serve others well
- Start with small, low-risk boundaries to build confidence
- Review the boundary scripts regularly until they feel natural

"I can't stick to anything consistently"

- Make your starting habit smaller (2 minutes instead of 10)
- Focus on one letter at a time for a full week
- Track your progress visually to maintain motivation

"My life is too chaotic for this system"

- Use the method as a compass, not a rigid schedule
- Focus on the "When You Feel Overwhelmed" practice
- Adapt the practices to fit your unique circumstances

Remember: The IMBALANCE Method is designed to be flexible and responsive to your life. Use what works, adapt what doesn't, and always prioritize progress over perfection.

ABOUT THE AUTHOR

J. McCarthy, PhD, MBA (also known as Dr. Jay) is a behavioral researcher, educator, and leadership consultant with a passion for helping professionals and change-makers reclaim their time, energy, and purpose. With a PhD in Advanced Studies in Human Behavior, an MBA, and a BS in eMarketing, he brings a multidisciplinary lens to real-world challenges like occupational burnout, work-life imbalance, and emotional fatigue.

Dr. Jay's work draws from decades of experience across corporate, nonprofit, and educational spaces, with specialties in business analytics, instructional technology, and organizational health. He is a mentor to leaders, educators, coaches, and professionals seeking sustainable success without sacrificing their well-being.

Having personally navigated the pressure of high-stakes roles while raising a large family and overcoming a major health crisis, Dr. Jay writes from both lived experience and rigorous research. His writing is known for blending psychological insight with actionable tools, meeting readers at the intersection of personal growth and professional excellence.

When he's not coaching, consulting, or creating transformational content, Dr. Jay resides in the Dallas-Fort Worth area with his wife of over 25 years and their seven children. His books are a testament to what's possible when clarity, strategy, and inner alignment come together.

ALSO AVAILABLE FROM
THE REAL LIFE SERIES PUBLISHING CO.

Managing the Imbalance: Behind the Whistle
Coaching Others Without Compromising Yourself
by J. McCarthy, PhD, MBA
ISBN: 979-8-9989754-7-9

www.ingramcontent.com/pod-product-compliance
Lightning Source LLC
Chambersburg PA
CBHW031423120626
46545CB00006B/2248